La Vergne Public Library
La Vergne, TN 37086

VIEWS ON SLAVERY

IN THE WORDS OF ENSLAVED
AFRICANS, MERCHANTS,
OWNERS, AND ABOLITIONISTS

SLAVERY AND SLAVE RESISTANCE

VIEWS ON SLAVERY

IN THE WORDS OF ENSLAVED AFRICANS, MERCHANTS, OWNERS, AND ABOLITIONISTS

SUZANNE CLOUD TAPPER

E **Enslow Publishing**
101 W. 23rd Street
Suite 240
New York, NY 10011
USA

enslow.com

Published in 2017 by Enslow Publishing, LLC
101 W. 23rd Street, Suite 240, New York, NY 10011

Copyright © 2017 by Suzanne Cloud Tapper

All rights reserved.

No part of this book may be reproduced by any means without the written permission of the publisher.

Library of Congress Cataloging-in-Publication Data
Names: Cloud Tapper, Suzanne, author.
Title: Views on slavery : in the words of enslaved Africans, merchants, owners, and abolitionists / Suzanne Cloud Tapper
Description: New York, NY : Enslow Publishing, 2017. | Series: Slavery and slave resistance | Includes bibliographical references and index.
Identifiers: LCCN 2015050585 | ISBN 9780766075535 (library bound)
Subjects: LCSH: Slavery--United States--History--Juvenile literature. | African Americans--History--To 1863--Juvenile literature.
Classification: LCC E441 .C595 2017 | DDC 306.3/620973--dc23
LC record available at http://lccn.loc.gov/2015050585

Printed in the United States of America

To Our Readers: We have done our best to make sure all website addresses in this book were active and appropriate when we went to press. However, the author and the publisher have no control over and assume no liability for the material available on those websites or on any websites they may link to. Any comments or suggestions can be sent by e-mail to customerservice@enslow.com.

Portions of this book appeared in the book *Voices From Slavery's Past: Yearning to be Heard*.

Photo Credits: Cover and throughout the book (Frederick Douglass), pp. 3, 10–11, 14–15, 58, 89, 98–99 Everett Historical/Shutterstock.com; Seregam/Shutterstock.com (chains used throughout the book); Digiselector/Shutterstock.com (series logo); pp. 8, 90–91 MPI/Archive Photos/Getty Images; pp. 18–19, 41, 42–43, 60–61, 72–73 © North Wind Picture Archives; p. 22 Hulton Archive/Archive Photos/Getty Images; p. 24 The Print Collector/Hulton Archive/Getty Images; pp. 26–27 Richard Worth; pp. 28–29 Time Life Pictures/Mansell/Life Picture Collection/Getty Images; pp. 34–35, 82 Library of Congress, Prints and Photographs Division; p, 37 DeAgostini/Getty Images; p. 45 Enslow Publishing, LLC; pp. 46–47 North Wind Picture Archives/Alamy; p. 49 from Josiah Clark Nott and George Robert Gliddon's "Indigenous Races of the Earth"/ (First published 1857)/ Wikimedia Commons/Races and skulls.png/public domain; p. 52 Popular Science Monthly Volume 65/Wikimedia Commons/PSM V65 D382 Joseph Le Conte.png/public domain; p. 63 Documenting the American South, University of North Carolina at Chapel Hill Library; p. 68 "Harriet Jacobs" By Jean Fagan Yellin/Wikimedia Commons/Harriet Ann Jacobs1894.png/public domain; p. 75 Hulton Archive/Getty Images; p. 77 Beinecke Rare Book & Manuscript Library, Yale University/ Wikimedia Commons/Remember Your Weekly Pledge Massachusetts Anti-Slavey Society collection box.jpg/public domain; p. 86 Garrison/Wikimedia Commons/1831 Liberator.jpg/public domain; pp. 100–101 Kena Betancur/AFP/Getty Images; pp. 102–103 Russell Lee/Library Of Congress/Getty Images; pp. 104–105 Francis Miller/The LIFE Picture Collection/Getty Images.

CONTENTS

CHAPTER 1
ESCAPE TO FREEDOM...**7**

CHAPTER 2
SLAVE MERCHANT TO AMAZING GRACE.............**21**

CHAPTER 3
GOODBYE TO AFRICA, MY HOME........................**33**

CHAPTER 4
SCIENCE AND RACISM..**45**

CHAPTER 5
PAMPERED BLINDNESS..**57**

CHAPTER 6
DESPERATE TO LIVE FREE....................................**67**

CHAPTER 7
FREEDOM'S HEROES...**80**

CHAPTER 8
"WE ARE THE CHANGE THAT WE SEEK"...........**95**

TIMELINE...**108**
CHAPTER NOTES..**111**
GLOSSARY..**121**
FURTHER READING..**123**
INDEX..**125**

CHAPTER 1

ESCAPE TO FREEDOM

Before Henry Bibb could scramble over the fence, his pursuers grabbed his legs and threatened to shoot him if he kept trying to run. He kicked at them and punched one of the men hard in the eye, but the crowd, wielding clubs and guns, was too much for Henry. They seized him, almost choking him to death. Then, they dragged him through the streets of Cincinnati, Ohio, to the Office of Justice. Henry would write later in his famous narrative that, "It was more like an office of injustice."[1] It was 1838, and Henry Bibb was a runaway slave. He would be taken back to the plantation of William Gatewood, located in the slave state of Kentucky.

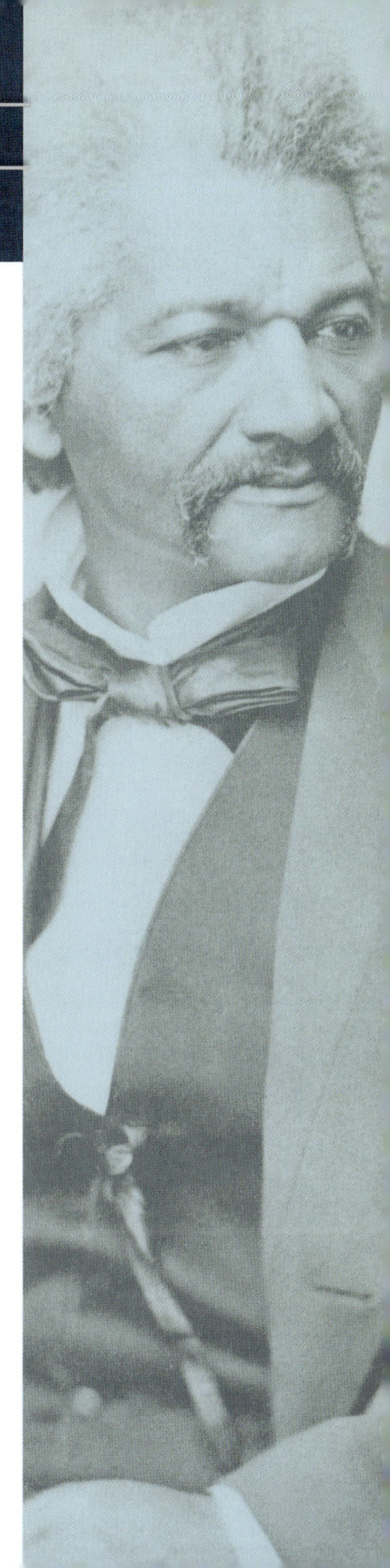

Henry Bibb was born into slavery but escaped to freedom in Canada. Through lectures and writing, Bibb became an influential abolitionist figure.

BORN INTO SLAVERY

Henry Bibb was born in 1815, the eldest son of a slave and her owner. He never knew his father because Henry was sold and taken away from his mother when he was very young. His life was filled with backbreaking work. Like most slaves, he worked from very early in the morning until late at night. He was always hungry because there was never enough to eat. When he did finally get to lie down, his bed was a cold bench without even a blanket to cover himself.[2] If he protested his harsh treatment in any way, Henry would feel the whip against his back from the overseer, who ran the plantation for the owner.

Henry decided when he was ten years old, to try and run away to freedom in the North every chance he got. Henry had talked about the North with other slaves and overheard whites talking among themselves. He said, "I learned the art of running away to perfection. I made a regular business of it, and never gave it up until I had broken the bands of slavery, and landed myself safely in Canada, where I was regarded as a man, and not as a thing."[3]

For a young slave boy or girl, dreaming of freedom was a dangerous thing, because trying to escape could mean death. Most slaves did not know geography outside their plantation. They had no means of transportation since a slave could not get on a boat or a train without permission papers from his or her owner. Travel was mostly done at night. Runaway slaves had little money or food. An escaped slave was always on the lookout for people likely to betray him or her to the local authorities. Because laws were passed that forbade slaves to read and write, many slaves did not understand road signs or even a "Wanted" poster nailed to a tree by slave hunters.

Slave hunters were bands of local men armed with weapons who rode through the countryside making sure the slaves stayed on their plantations. They would beat, torture, and sometimes kill runaway slaves. On the trek north, frightened slaves would be listening intently for the slave hunters' ferocious hounds. Each day might bring capture and a return to the dreaded master with his whip.[4]

VIEWS ON SLAVERY: IN THE WORDS OF ENSLAVED AFRICANS, MERCHANTS, OWNERS, AND ABOLITIONISTS

Slaves who tried to flee risked everything. Runaway slaves who were found, which was more likely than not, were subject to harsh physical abuse and even death.

JUMPING THE BROOM

In 1833, when Henry Bibb was eighteen years old, he met a girl named Malinda. She was a slave who worked on the nearby Gatewood plantation.[5] Bibb would often leave his master's house without permission to see Malinda. Upon returning, he would be flogged for being away without a pass. Many slaves in Antebellum America would run away for short periods of time to rejoin family that had been sold to other slaveholders. Most white owners did not care if husbands were separated from wives or mothers from their babies.[6] Bibb endured each beating until his owner, tiring of the troublesome slave, decided to give in and sell Henry Bibb to Malinda's master, William Gatewood.

Malinda and Henry wanted to marry, but slaves were not allowed to legally wed. So, they would have ceremonies on their own. Just saying out loud to everyone that they were married made it so. Sometimes, they would even "jump the broom." A broom would be held about a foot off the floor and the couple would jump over it. Once they jumped, they were married in the eyes of the slave community.[7]

A LITTLE GIRL BEATEN

After a while, Malinda and Henry Bibb had a lovely daughter named Mary Frances. They were happy until Henry realized that he was powerless to help his family whenever their masters would beat them.

One day, while Malinda and Henry were working in the fields, the mistress of the plantation beat their little girl so severely that she had a large welt on the side of her face. When Henry saw this, he knew he had to try and escape and then later bring his family to freedom. He wrote, "It required all the moral courage that I was master of to suppress my feeling while taking leave of my little family."[8]

LEAVING GATEWOOD PLANTATION

On Christmas in 1837, Henry Bibb got a pass from William Gatewood to try and find work nearby. Sometimes when the workload on a plantation slowed, owners would hire out some of their slaves to be employed by local businesses. They also took

> Henry Bibb described how poor, white laborers in the South secretly wanted slavery abolished:
>
> *The slave holders are generally rich, aristocratic, overbearing; and they look with utter contempt upon a poor laboring man, who earns his bread by the "sweat of his brow," whether he be moral or immoral, honest or dishonest. No matter whether he is white or black; if he performs manual labor for a livelihood, he is looked upon as being inferior to a slaveholder, and but little better off than the slave, who toils without wages under the lash. It is true, that the slaveholder, and non-slaveholder, are living under the same laws in the same State. But the one is rich, the other is poor; one is educated, the other is uneducated; one has houses, land and influence, the other has none. This being the case, that class of the non-slaveholders would be glad to see slavery abolished, but they dare not speak it aloud.* [9]

whatever money the slave earned.[10] Bibb used this ruse to catch a steamboat to Perrysburgh, Ohio, where he found work.[11] He worked all winter and met some abolitionists who aided him in his desire to bring his family north. They were worried when he insisted on going back to Kentucky for his wife and daughter. His friends were sure that Gatewood would be searching for him. Henry Bibb did not listen. He went back in May of 1837 to get them and take them to Canada.[12]

CAPTURED!

Bibb made it back to Gatewood Plantation undetected and secretly met Malinda to give her money for steamboat passage to Cincinnati. She promised she would see him the next Sunday.[13] She did not make it. Her owners lied to her and told her that the abolitionists had promised to help her husband, but then had sold Henry to slaveholders in New Orleans. This frightened her. Slaves who were sold "down river" to Louisiana rarely escaped again. The swampy climate and working conditions were too brutal.[14]

Henry Bibb and his abolitionist friends started arranging for passage to Lake Erie for Henry's family. At this time, American abolitionists were using the Underground Railroad to help slaves escape to freedom. There were stations, or safe houses, where runaway slaves could be hidden from the slave hunters. Runaway slaves needed food, clothing, and money. So, abolitionists raised money from antislavery groups who wanted to help.[15]

Unfortunately for Bibb, informants hired by Gatewood's slave hunters pretended they were abolitionists. They told the slave hunters where he was. He bolted and tried to climb a fence to get away. They caught him and locked him up in the local jail. Henry Bibb later wrote, "This was the first time in my life that I had been put into a jail. It was truly distressing to my feelings to be locked up in a cold dungeon for no crime."[16]

The slave hunters thought that Bibb could tell them the whereabouts of other runaway slaves. He refused, replying:

> No, gentlemen, I cannot commit or do an act of that kind . . . I know that I am now in the power of the master who can sell me from my family for life, or punish me for the crime of running away . . . I also know that I have been deceived and betrayed by men who professed to be my best friends; but can all this justify me in becoming a traitor to others?[17]

ESCAPE TO FREEDOM

SOLD AT THE SLAVE MARKET

Miraculously, Henry Bibb escaped and made it back to his wife, daughter, and mother in secret. His mother found someone who could hide her son. Henry Bibb wrote that, "The next day after my arrival . . . [they] came to the very house wherein I was concealed and talked in my hearing to the family about my escape . . . He was near enough for me to have laid my hands on his head while in that house."[18] Fearing

This engraving from the book, *Narrative of the Life and Adventures of Henry Bibb, An American Slave*, shows Bibb being captured with another fugitive slave named Jack from Louisiana.

that the reward for him would tempt people to turn him in, Henry Bibb told his family that he had to leave again and try to get to Ohio. Sadly, Bibb was betrayed again, by the people hiding him, for a five-dollar reward.

"Shoot him down! Shoot him down! If he offers to run or resist, kill him!" the slave hunters cried as they surrounded Henry Bibb.[19] They tied his hands behind him and robbed him of his money, a silver watch, a pocketknife, and a Bible. Then, they chained his hands and feet with heavy irons.[20] William Gatewood, master of Henry, Malinda and Mary Frances Bibb, decided to sell the entire family at the slave market.

Eventually, Henry Bibb and his family were taken to New Orleans and sold to a man named Deacon Whitfield, who decided to split the family up. Henry Bibb wrote that, "This was truly heart-rending to my poor wife; the thought of our being torn apart in a strange land after having been sold away from all her friends and relations, was more than she could bear."[21]

IN THE SWAMPS

The family decided to escape. But the murky swamps of Louisiana were not the same as the rolling hills of Kentucky. The little family became lost in the muddy bayous of the Red River. Snakes and alligators were everywhere. They finally found themselves on a tiny island and quickly fell asleep, only to be awakened in the dead of night to the howling of wolves.[22]

Henry fought off the beasts. The family began to travel through the wilderness, not sure of where they were going. Soon, slave hunters' dogs were after them. Henry Bibb started to run with his little daughter in his arms, but he tripped and fell. Mary Frances got hurt and was bleeding heavily. But Bibb knew the running was over. "The dogs were soon at our heels, and we were compelled to stop or be torn to pieces by them."[23]

The next day, Henry was whipped and then fitted with a heavy iron collar with a long prong extending above his head with a bell on it. He was forced to wear this heavy load of iron for six weeks. Every night, he was chained to a log after working all day. Eventually, he was sold to some gamblers. As he left with his new owners, Henry could hear the horrified screams and weeping of Malinda and Mary Frances. He would never see them again.[24]

ESCAPE AND FIGHTING SLAVERY

Many slave families in the Antebellum South were considered property, nothing more, and they were forced to live and work their entire lives at the whim of white plantation owners and their families. Henry Bibb did escape again. He taught himself to read and write, and he became a member of the abolitionist movement. He lectured around the country, informing people of the horrors of slavery. He wrote the following at the beginning of his 1849 autobiography:

> I have been educated in the school of adversity, whips, and chains . . . to be changed from a chattel to a human being is no light matter . . . if I could reach the ears of every slave today throughout the whole continent of America, I would teach the same lesson . . . "break your chains and fly for freedom!" [25]

SLAVERY IN THE UNITED STATES

Henry Bibb's personal story illustrates one man's viewpoint of the institution of slavery in America—that of the slaves living under the domination of a harsh white society. The first slaves arrived in the British colonies in the early 1600s, and slavery did not officially end until Congress passed the Thirteenth Amendment in 1865. Usually, the people chosen to be slaves had dark skin. These people were

VIEWS ON SLAVERY: IN THE WORDS OF ENSLAVED AFRICANS, MERCHANTS, OWNERS, AND ABOLITIONISTS

kept in substandard housing, underfed, uneducated, and worked hard their entire lives. They were supposed to obey their owners without question.

As time went on, the slave trade developed a triangular pattern. Goods were shipped from England to Africa and were traded for slaves who were then taken to America or the West Indies. The slave ships would then return to England with produce or money. Many white people of the time felt that slavery was a good thing. Others worked very hard to end slavery. By the early 1800s, abolitionists had helped to end most slavery in the northern United States. The southern states refused to give up their slaves though, and this disagreement resulted in a bloody Civil War between the North and the South from 1861 to 1865.

This resource contains the personal stories of people who were very involved in slavery. There is one account of a slave trader and one of the daughter of a slave owner. There is a tale of a slave woman who hid herself for seven years just to be

---

African slaves had a long history in America. The first slaves were brought from Africa to the Jamestown colony in the 1600s. This was the beginning of a profitable and inhumane slave trade.

free. Another account describes two famous abolitionists who tirelessly fought the negative attitudes held by whites toward African Americans. All of these people have a unique story to tell about slavery. All of them have views that were carefully shaped by their experiences. The institution of slavery deeply affected the United States, and its legacy is still with us today. In this book, individuals tell their own history as *they* saw it. And often, the stories people tell themselves are the most powerful of all.

CHAPTER 2

SLAVE MERCHANT TO AMAZING GRACE

When John Newton was twenty years old, he found himself in slavery on an island off the coast of Sierra Leone in Africa. Newtown came from a wealthy English family. His father, an important master of ships, had hoped John would make a fine sailor someday, but Newton was a high-spirited young man who got into trouble early in his career at sea. One day, his captain became so angry, he kicked Newton off the ship and he ended up at the mercy of a white slave dealer named Clow and his African wife.[1]

JOHN NEWTON.

John Newton had the distinction of working on a slave ship before being captured into slavery himself. Once free, Newton continued to work in the slave trade until renouncing it for religious reasons.

WHITE SLAVERY

Newton was forced to work long hours on a lime plantation. He wrote later that his "bed was a mat spread upon a board . . . and a log of wood my pillow."[2] He never had enough to eat and had to dig up roots for sustenance. In the hot and humid weather of Sierra Leone, English people died easily of dehydration, heat exhaustion, and diseases such as yellow fever and malaria. Newton complained that his only clothes were "a shirt, a pair of trousers, a cotton handkerchief instead of a cap."[3] For months, it rained off and on all day and night. Newton would feel the drops falling on his head, running down his face and into his eyes. He never felt dry. Because of the continuous dampness, Newton became very ill and almost did not survive.[4]

A FATHER SEARCHES FOR HIS SON

His father had been looking for his lost son and asked many captains to inquire about him in all their ports of call. At last, *The Greyhound* found him. John was thankful that his horrifying ordeal as someone's slave was over, but the experience did not make Newton condemn slavery. In 1750, when he was twenty-five years old, Newton became a slave trader of his own ship, the *Duke of Argyle*.

At the time, slavery was very important to the English and American economic systems. Big companies like the Dutch West India Company and the English Royal African Company had investors in Europe and America who wanted to make money from selling sugar and rum, but mostly money was made from selling and transporting slaves.[5] The people who paid for the slave ships were only concerned with profit. They did not feel that buying and selling human beings was wrong. A small religious group called the Quakers were against slavery, but most white people accepted it without question. And John Newton was no exception. Despite his own experience, he did not feel that slavery was an institution that was morally reprehensible.

This page from John Newton's journal while at sea suggests what little regard he likely held for the slaves onboard. He notes the deaths of two slaves and refers to them only by number.

HOW WHITES VIEWED AFRICANS

Of course, Newton felt enslaving Englishmen was a crime. But much of the white world viewed Africans as less than human. Putting Africans in chains, however, was just good business. On board his ship, Newton referred to his white crew as people, while the Africans in his care were assigned numbers.[6] According to Newton, the slaves believed in magic and witchcraft. He did not understand that African religions, languages, and traditions were very different from the beliefs he was taught as a child. All sea captains had to keep a daily journal during each voyage and, one day in 1753, Newton wrote:

> The three greatest blessings of which human nature is capable are . . . religion, liberty and love. In each of these how highly has God distinguished me! But here in Africa are whole nations around me, whose languages . . . have no words among them . . . [for] these engaging ideas.[7]

THE TRIANGLE TRADE

To Newton and other slave traders, African people were just cargo to be taken across the sea and sold in the Triangle Trade. One side of the triangle was the trip from England to the West Coast of Africa. Ships carried cargoes of cloth, guns, alcohol, and other items that the English knew the slave dealers wanted. When the ships arrived, they cast off their longboats to sail up and down the coast along many rivers and creeks searching for slaves to capture or buy. This was called the coasting period, and it often lasted six to eight months. The second side of the triangle, between Africa and the American colonies, was called the Middle Passage. This trip took about two months, depending on the weather. When they reached North America, the slaves were sold to white plantation owners. The last side of the triangle was the homeward trip back to England. The ship sometimes carried cotton, sugar, tobacco, or rum. However, money was the chief cargo and it

VIEWS ON SLAVERY: IN THE WORDS OF ENSLAVED AFRICANS, MERCHANTS, OWNERS, AND ABOLITIONISTS

Triangular Trade

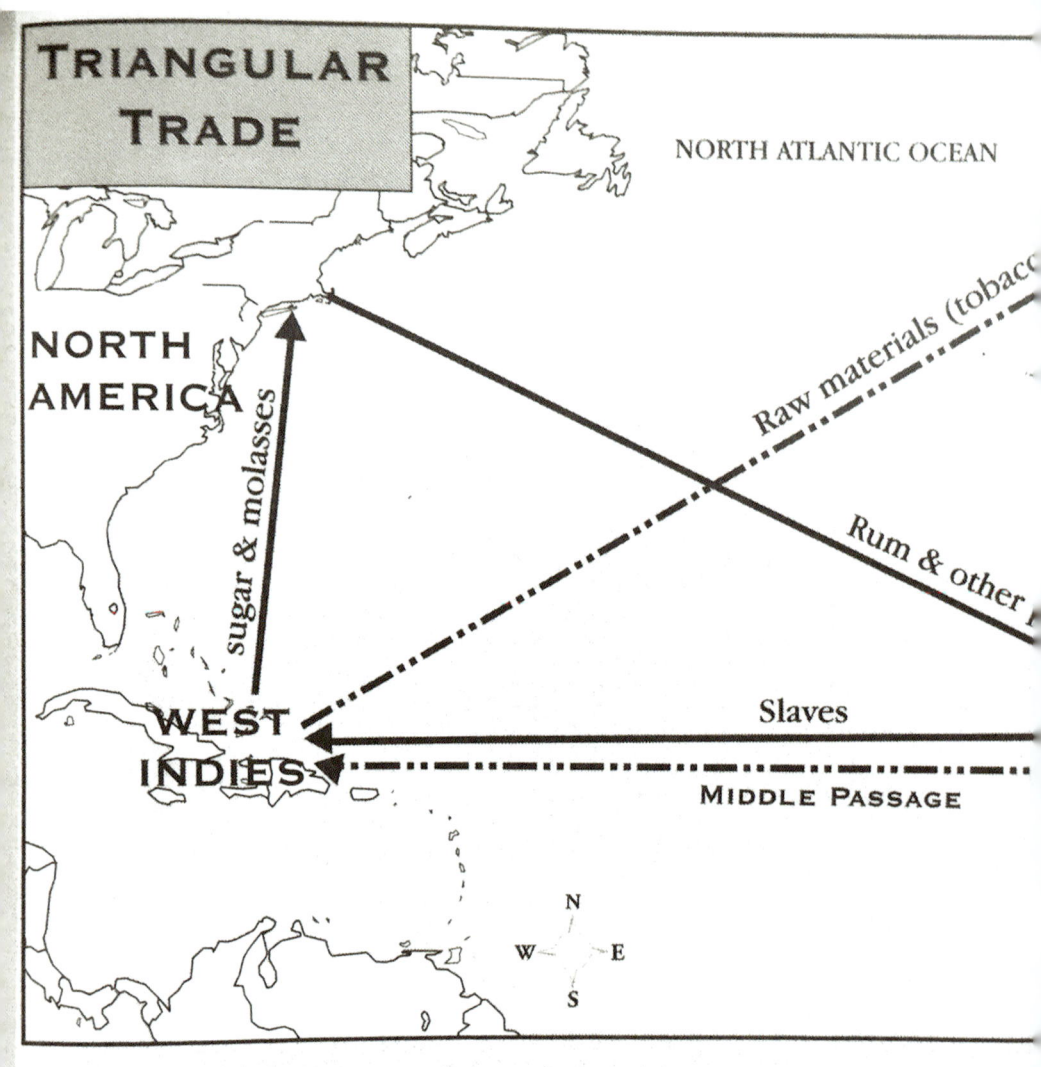

- NORTH ATLANTIC OCEAN
- NORTH AMERICA
- WEST INDIES
- sugar & molasses
- Raw materials (tobacc...
- Rum & other
- Slaves
- MIDDLE PASSAGE

The sale of slaves to the New World was just part of the vast triangular trade that involved many different countries

> The sale of slaves to North America was just part of the vast triangular trade that involved many countries. It was an efficient system designed to exchange goods and slaves.

26

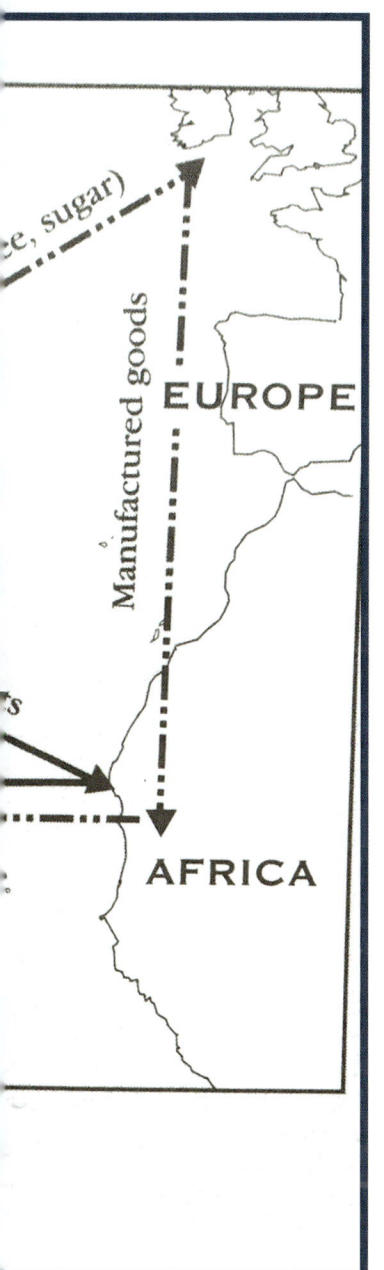

lined the pockets of the captain and the ship owners.[8] When the slave trade was going strongest in the 1700s, about 6 million Africans were taken across the Atlantic Ocean. Over 54,000 voyages were made in 300 years of slave trading.[9]

CROSSING THE OCEAN

A slave trader's main goal was getting as many living slaves to America as possible. Men, women, and children were packed on their sides below decks, unable to stand or even sit up.[10] Because captains were constantly afraid of slaves rising up against them, which happened quite often, the male slaves were kept under heavy guard and in chains most of the time. The women and children were also frequently chained to prevent them from throwing themselves overboard. John Newton wrote of the space allotted on his ships for the slaves:

> The space between decks was five feet. . . . The slaves were chained in couples, right hand and right foot of one to the left of the other and so stowed upon the platform and the deck below—their headroom being rather less than thirty inches.[11]

If a slave was put on the ship at the beginning of the coasting period, it is

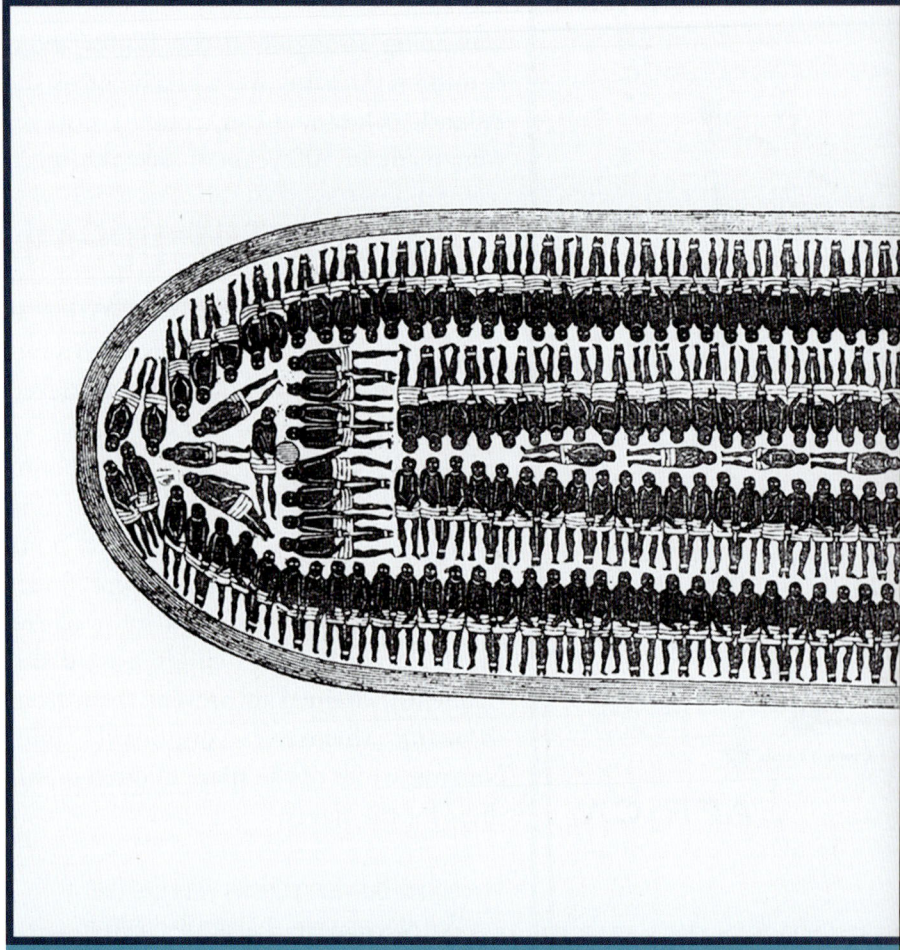

VIEWS ON SLAVERY: IN THE WORDS OF ENSLAVED AFRICANS, MERCHANTS, OWNERS, AND ABOLITIONISTS

This drawing of the interior of a slave ship illustrates the method used to transport a maximum number of slaves. The kidnapped Africans were packed tightly, with little room to move or breathe.

possible that he or she could spend eight months on board a ship with very little chance to walk around, get fresh air, or feel the sun on his or her face. Below decks, it was always dirty and smelly from so many

SLAVE MERCHANT TO AMAZING GRACE

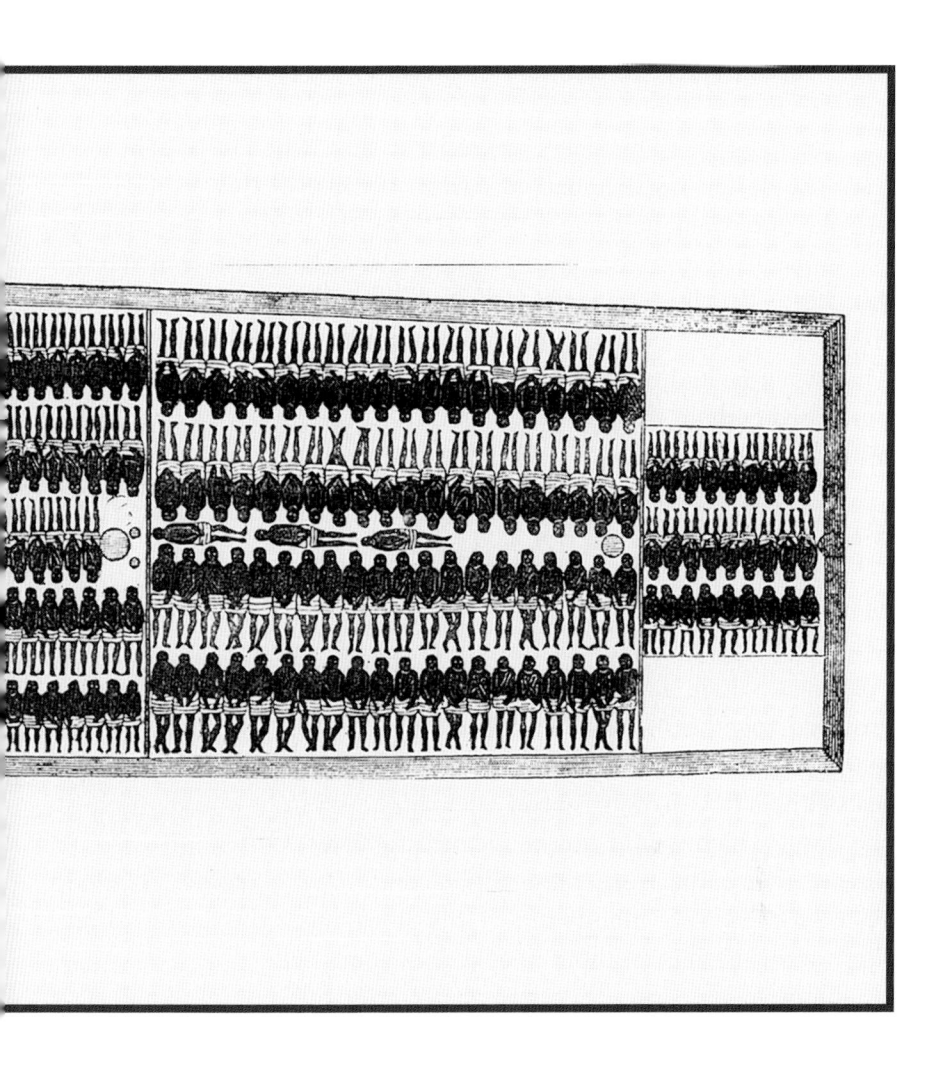

people living in such a small place. Newton felt that some people died of heartache. He wrote in his journal:

> Wednesday 9th January . . . This day buried a fine woman slave. No. 11, having been ailing some time, but never thought

her in danger till within these last 2 days; she was taken with a lethargick [sic] disorder, which they seldom recover from.[12]

Newton gave all his slaves a number to show when he bought them from the dealers on the coast of Africa. Because of this, it is possible to find out when he bought No. 11. On the 19th of the previous November, Newton "bought a woman and a slave girl" (No. 11 and No. 12).[13] This means that No. 11 had been a captive on the *Duke of Argyle* for 51 days. Newton's ship did not leave the coast of Africa until May, when he had filled his hold with at least 250 slaves, so the slaves purchased early in the coasting period had been mostly chained up in his hold for six months.

THE MIDDLE PASSAGE

Many slaves died as a result of the miserable conditions during the Middle Passage to America. In rough seas, the small windows, called portholes, which gave fresh air to the hold where the Africans were crowded together, would be closed tight. It then became hot, and many people died from suffocation. Most of the slaves suffered from sea sickness (few had ever been on a ship), and they would vomit on the floor, which would not be cleaned for days. Others died from a disease that came from these filthy conditions: a sickness Captain Newton called the "bloody flux." This illness made the slave area very dirty and caused even more people to become sick.

Between the slave dealers in the interior of Africa and the slave traders buying Africans on the coast and taking them to the other side of the ocean, the death toll was frighteningly high. Out of every 100 people kidnapped in Africa and sold to slave dealers, 57 would reach the coast to be bought by slave traders and board the ships. Of those 57 who survived the trip over land, 51 would make it across the ocean. Only about 48 would eventually be sold in the New World.[14] Fewer than half of the initial 100 people would survive. And the life that awaited them in America was no better.

> In *Thoughts Upon the African Slave Trade*, John Newton describes how the horrible conditions below a slave ship's deck often proved fatal for the African captives:
>
> *If the slaves and their rooms can be constantly aired, and they are not detained too long on board, perhaps there are not many who die; but the contrary is often their lot. They are kept down, by the weather, to breathe a hot and corrupted air, sometimes for a week: this added to the galling of their irons, and the despondency which seizes their spirits when thus confined, soon becomes fatal. And every morning, perhaps, more instances than one are found, of the living and the dead . . .*[15]

NEWTON TURNS AGAINST SLAVERY

John Newton would make three voyages as a slave trader, which was typical of a slave ship captain. Later he would write, "my heart now shudders"[16] at the fact that he was involved in buying and selling human beings. Unlike nearly all other slave traders, John Newton grew to believe that slavery was wrong. He wrote "What I did, I did ignorantly."[17]

This kind of blindness to the cruelty of slavery was very common. If people are told that someone who is different from themselves is not human, they will come to believe it. If they read it in books, or are told this over and over again, they will come to accept it as truth. Captain John Newton was one of the few slave traders who eventually understood that just because everyone says something is right and

VIEWS ON SLAVERY: IN THE WORDS OF ENSLAVED AFRICANS, MERCHANTS, OWNERS, AND ABOLITIONISTS

good, does not necessarily make it so. Later, he became a priest for the Church of England and wrote many hymns, including the famous song "Amazing Grace," which is still sung today. The first verse tells the story of how someone can come to see things in a different light:

> *Amazing Grace, how sweet the sound*
> *That saved a wretch like me*
> *I once was lost, but now I'm found*
> *Was blind, but now I see.*

In 1755, John Newton gave up the slave trade for good. That same year, eleven-year-old Olaudah Equiano was taken from his home by Africans bent on selling him to Europeans on the coast. The Middle Passage brought many slaves from their homes in Africa to new lives of hard labor and abuse in North America.

CHAPTER 3

GOODBYE TO AFRICA, MY HOME

Ten year old Olaudah Equiano loved living in the home he called Essaka[1] in the kingdom of Benin, which is now known as southern Nigeria. He was a young Ibo boy who loved playing games with his brothers and his sister. Olaudah also enjoyed helping his father hunt and helping his mother tend their fields of yams, beans, and corn.[2] What was even more fun for him was celebrating the harvest with the whole village when the crops were ripe and freshly picked. Their supreme god Chukwu protected them, and his tribe was very grateful for the blessings that each year brought.[3] Olaudah wrote in his autobiography many years later about the joy of the celebration:

VIEWS ON SLAVERY: IN THE WORDS OF ENSLAVED AFRICANS, MERCHANTS, OWNERS, AND ABOLITIONISTS

The Interesting Narrative of the Life of Olaudah Equiano was published in 1794. Once free from slavery, Equiano educated abolitionists about the slave trade by sharing his harrowing experiences.

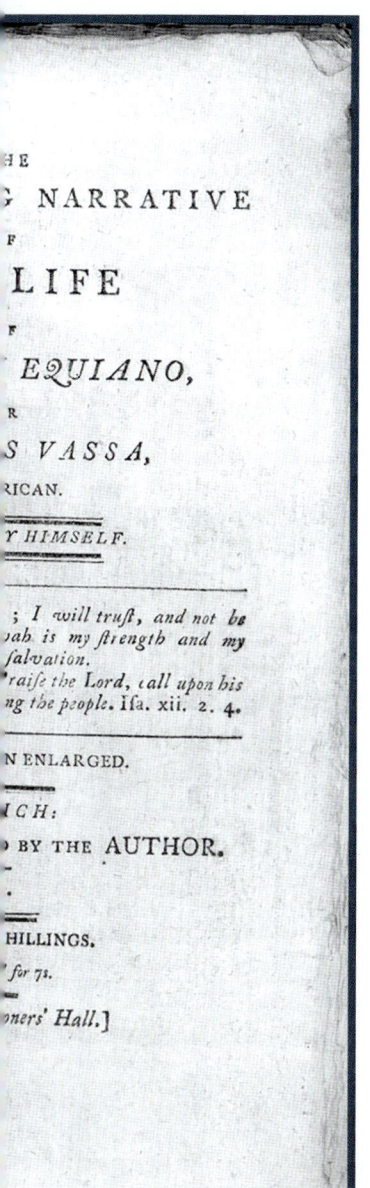

We are almost a nation of dancers, musicians and poets . . . every great event . . . is celebrated in public dances which are accompanied with songs and music. . . . We have many musical instruments, particularly drums of different kinds, . . . [something] which resembles a guitar [banjo] . . . and another much like a stickado [xylophone].

IBO JUSTICE

Slavery was not unknown to Olaudah Equiano. His father was an important man in the village, and owned slaves himself. In Ibo villages, there was no single king who ruled everyone. Decisions were made by councils of elders, a council of chiefs, women's groups, and secret societies.[4] The chief men of the Ibo tribe acted like judges to decide arguments among the people and punishments for criminals. One sentence for breaking the law was that the person could be sold to a neighboring tribe[5].

In Africa, slavery was thought to be serving others for a time. People felt it was more humane than jailing someone for many years or killing the person.[6] A slave would not be sent so far away from home that the person could never see his or her family again. Slaves were not treated as if they were not human. Many times, the slaves were adopted into their master's family. Lastly, they were not made slaves for life. Olaudah wrote in his book, "With us they do no more work than other members of the community, even their master . . . their food, clothing and lodging were nearly the same as theirs. . . . Some of these slaves have even slaves under them, as their own property, and for their own use."[7]

KIDNAPPED!

One day when Olaudah and his sister were left at home alone, two men and a woman came over the walls of their yard and seized them. "Without giving us time to cry out . . . they stopped our mouths and tied our hands and ran off with us."[8] Olaudah was taken from the

> Olaudah Equiano describes how a free black man was forced into slavery by a captain of a slaver:
> *There was a very clever and decent free young mulatto-man who sailed a long time with us: he had a free woman for his wife, by whom he had a child; and she was then living on shore, . . . all knew this young man from a child that he was always free, and no one had ever claimed him as their property: however, . . . a Bermudas captain, . . . came on board of us, and seeing the mulattoman, . . . told him he was not free, and that he had orders from his master to bring him to Bermudas. The poor man could not believe the captain to be in earnest; but he was very soon undeceived, his men laying violent hands on him: and although he shewed a certificate of his being born free in St. Kitt's, . . . he was taken forcibly out of our vessel. . . . the next day, without . . . or suffering him even to see his wife or child, he was carried away, and probably doomed never more in this world to see them again.*[9]

Maniere dont les Maures prennent les Esclaves.

Slave traders, often aided by local agents, traveled through African villages and kidnapped adults and children. The slaves were transported to America and sold, never to see their homes again.

interior of Africa, and he was sold over and over again to different families who, luckily, treated him well. But he was homesick. Olaudah had never been far away from home before.

He saw many strange and some pleasant things along the way, but when he came to a big river filled with canoes he was very afraid.

> I had never before seen any water larger than a pond . . . and my surprise was mingled with no small fear when I was put into one of theses canoes. . . . I continued to travel . . . through different countries and various nations, till at the end of six or seven months after I had been kidnapped. I arrived at the seacoast.[10]

SLAVE SHIP IN A HUGE OCEAN

The first thing that Olaudah saw when he reached the coast was the vast ocean and a huge slave ship at anchor. The sight must have made him feel very small. He was dragged on board by white men. Olaudah thought they were going to kill him.[11] The crew of the slave ship spoke in a language Olaudah had never heard. He did not understand what they were trying to tell him to do. He was pushed and shoved. Worst of all, they were very dirty and stinky. Olaudah had never seen people like this. His people were very clean and washed their hands before every meal. These men smelled of liquor and body odor.

> When I looked round the ship . . . and saw . . . a multitude of black people of every description chained together, every one of their [faces] expressing . . . sorrow, I no longer doubted of my fate . . . I fell motionless on the deck and fainted.[12]

When Olaudah awoke he asked some slaves around him, "Are we not to be eaten by those white men with the horrible looks, red faces, and long hair?"[13] They told him no. They told him the men would be taking him to work in the white man's land across the sea. What Olaudah did not know at this point was that he was about to voyage on the dreaded Middle Passage. He did not know about a land this far away from his home. He did not know that little boys like him were prized possessions of the slave traders. Boys like Olaudah were considered old enough to work like grown-ups and young enough to easily learn English. Young slaves were worth a lot of money. Proof of this would be seen many years later when the wreckage of the slave ship, the *Henrietta Marie*, would be brought up from the bottom of the ocean and one hundred pairs of shackles or handcuffs were found. They were forged just big enough for the wrists and ankles of children.[14]

LONELY AND AFRAID

Olaudah sank into despair because he knew that he had lost any chance of returning to Africa. Olaudah was a scared little boy. His family was gone, and he was alone. He could not understand what was being said to him or talk to the people in charge of him. New sights and smells were all around him and filled him with terror.

Olaudah was soon dragged below the ship's deck. The little boy was revolted by the stench that came up from the slave quarters and horrified by the cries of the people who were chained down there. "I became so sick and low that I was not able to eat, nor had I the least desire to taste anything. I now wished for the last friend, Death, to relieve me."[15] Olaudah refused to eat. This angered the slave ship's crew. To them, this young boy was worth too much money to let him starve himself. So they held him by the hands, laid him over a big crank on the ship, tied his feet and whipped him until he screamed. Olaudah wrote later that, even though he was very afraid of the water, if he could have gotten over the ropes on the sides of the ship, "I would have jumped over the side."[16]

Because the ship was in its coasting period and Olaudah was a young boy, he was allowed to stay on deck in the fresh air most of the time. His captors did not see him as a threat. When the ship finally set sail for the Middle Passage, Olaudah was once again put below deck.

VIEWS ON SLAVERY: IN THE WORDS OF ENSLAVED AFRICANS, MERCHANTS, OWNERS, AND ABOLITIONISTS

> The closeness of the place, and the heat of the climate, added to the number in the ship, which was so crowded that each had scarcely room to turn himself, almost suffocated us . . . the shrieks of the women, and the groans of the dying tendered the whole a scene of horror almost inconceiveable [sic].[17]

SLAVES KILL THEMSELVES

Many slaves died during the trip, so the slave traders would cram too many people into the hold to make up for the ones who would die on the journey. This caused much suffering and even more death.

To try and keep the adult slaves alive, the crew would bring them up on deck for short periods of time. Olaudah was able to see some of what the other slaves endured. Many wanted to starve themselves, and he saw the slaves whipped for not eating. Other times, lips would be burned with a hot coal or molten lead would be poured on the skin to force the slaves to eat.[18] One day, Olaudah witnessed a suicide.

> We had a smooth sea . . . two of my wearied countrymen, who were chained together (I was near them at the time), preferring death to such a life of misery . . . jumped into the sea . . . and I believe many more would very soon have done the same if they had not been prevented by the ship's crew. [19]

Africans aboard slave ships did not have many ways to resist their captors. It was just too difficult. Some tried to jump into the ocean. Others tried to take over the ship. Both types of resistance were seen as slave revolts. Both were harshly dealt with by the captains and crew.

Captured slaves did what they could to escape their fate. Some attempted mutinies. Others jumped overboard, choosing death to a life of enslavement.

COMING TO BARBADOS

Finally, Olaudah Equiano reached the end of his voyage and the ship pulled into the harbor of the island of Barbados. When they anchored, Olaudah described how the merchants and planters boarded the ship and rushed toward the Africans. The strange men made them jump up and down to see if the slaves were healthy and poked them all over their bodies. Olaudah wrote, "And [then they] pointed to land, signifying we were to go there. We thought by this we should be eaten by these ugly men."[20] Later on, Olaudah and the other slaves were sold in the marketplace. In his autobiography, Olaudah described the sale and called it "the scramble," with loved ones and relatives being separated, never to see each other again. He later added:

> On a signal given (as the beat of a drum), the buyers rush at once into the yard where the slaves are confined and make a choice of [what] they like best. The noise. . . and the eagerness visible in the [faces] of the buyers . . . increase the apprehensions of the terrified Africans. . . . [21]

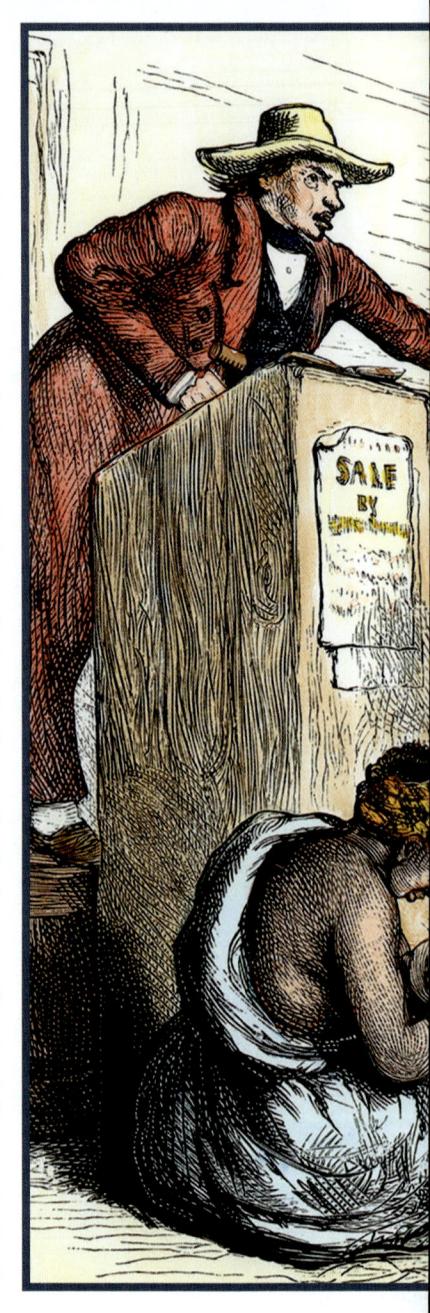

GOODBYE TO AFRICA, MY HOME

Once in America, the captured Africans were cleaned up and sold at auction. During the degrading process of being sold, slaves were treated like livestock, and many families were torn apart.

A few days later, Olaudah Equiano was taken to Virginia where he was sold to a local planter. He was only there a few months when a British officer in the navy bought him and took him to England to be his aide. Olaudah would eventually fight in the French and Indian War and would later work on slave ships himself until he was able to buy his freedom in 1766.[22]

RACIST BELIEFS

Many European and American scientists of the time believed that the way people looked determined what they were like inside. These men thought that the color of someone's skin or the shape of someone's eyes was proof of inferiority or superiority. To them, humanity was divided into racial groups that went from higher to lower on a scale of worth. White Europeans considered themselves to be the most superior. Africans were thought to be the most inferior. Equiano, unfortunately, was an African Ibo boy.

Olaudah Equiano's story has been challenged by some historians. Some say that it is not completely true. People telling their own personal stories usually leave out parts or put in parts that are not exactly factual. Slave stories give us an idea of what it must have been like to live as a slave. As one can see, Equiano's view of slavery was much different from the white Europeans' of the day.

Olaudah Equiano would eventually become a leading figure in the abolitionist movement, and millions would read about his life in the years to come. But he would never know what happened to his little sister or see his parents again.

CHAPTER 4

SCIENCE AND RACISM

Joseph Le Conte was born on a plantation in Liberty County, Georgia in 1823. About 200 slaves were forced to work for Joseph and his family. As a boy, Joseph was friendly to many of them. Daddy Dick was a slave and the family gardener who helped Joseph's father create a beautiful botanical garden. These two men worked closely together to create new types of plant life. People from all over the world would visit the family garden and marvel at the wonders in it and the talents of the growers.

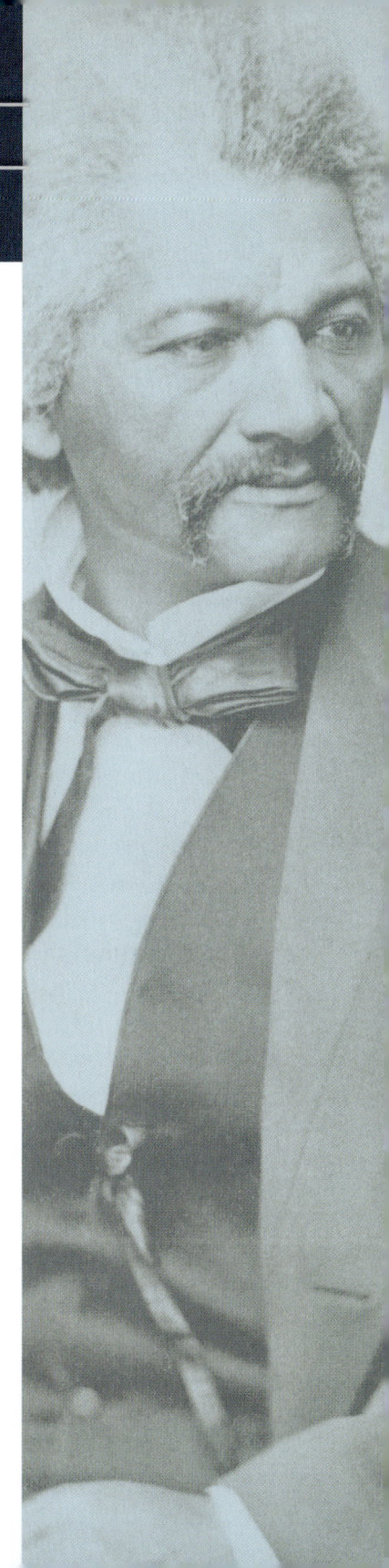

Le Conte wrote in his autobiography that his experience in the garden as a young boy would inspire him to become a scientist later in life.[1] Joseph had been taught by his father that although Daddy Dick was intelligent, he had to be constantly supervised. This was because his skin was dark. Nearly every white person in Joseph's neighborhood and nearly every white person that he ever met felt the same way.²

TOTAL CONTROL OF ANOTHER PERSON

Even though they might really like their slaves, many southern whites were comfortable telling slaves what to do. Even a small boy or girl could totally control a slave! A young boy like Joseph could beat a slave any time he felt like it and no one would say anything. He might tell his father that a slave refused to do something. His father might then give the slave a beating. Because of this, most slaves were very careful to always smile in front of white people so they would not be mistreated. As a result, slave owners began to believe that black people were very happy to be slaves. Joseph grew up thinking that all slaves enjoyed working hard for no pay. Le Conte saw slaves, young and old, laboring to grow rice and cotton on his plantation, Woodmanston. However, Le Conte believed that, "The negroes themselves enjoyed it hugely."³ This idea was part of a belief system called polygenism.

SCIENCE AND RACISM

Slaves were trained to be polite and deferential to whites. They knew the punishments that awaited them if they appeared unhappy or ungrateful.

> In describing his father's "moral character," Joseph Le Conte depicts the slaves on their plantation and throughout the county as happy. In reality, slaves were not that happy and faked looking happy because some overseers would beat slaves if they were not smiling.
>
> *But in moral character he was no less remarkable. Indeed the best qualities of character were constantly exercised and cultivated in the just, wise, and kindly management of his two hundred slaves. The negroes were strongly attached to him, and proud of calling him master.*
>
> *... There never was a more orderly, nor apparently a happier, working class than the negroes of Liberty County as I knew them in my boyhood.*[4]

THE GREAT CHAIN OF BEING

Polygenism was an idea that became very popular while Joseph Le Conte was going to school, but it was an old concept. One of Le Conte's teachers, Louis Agassiz, was one of polygenism's chief backers in America. This belief system held that a divine being had created each group on earth separately and that instead of one human race, there were three: whites, Asians, and blacks. Many scientists thought that the physical differences in people were directly connected to their intelligence and ability. For example, since Asians had eyes that looked slanted and they appeared to be looking out of the corner of their eyes, they were considered to be sneaky and tricky.[5] Some people believed that certain groups were better than others and that God had ranked the groups in a special order of value from highest to lowest. Many scientists called it "The Great Chain of Being." According to many white people in the 1800s, Asians, Hispanics, American Indians,

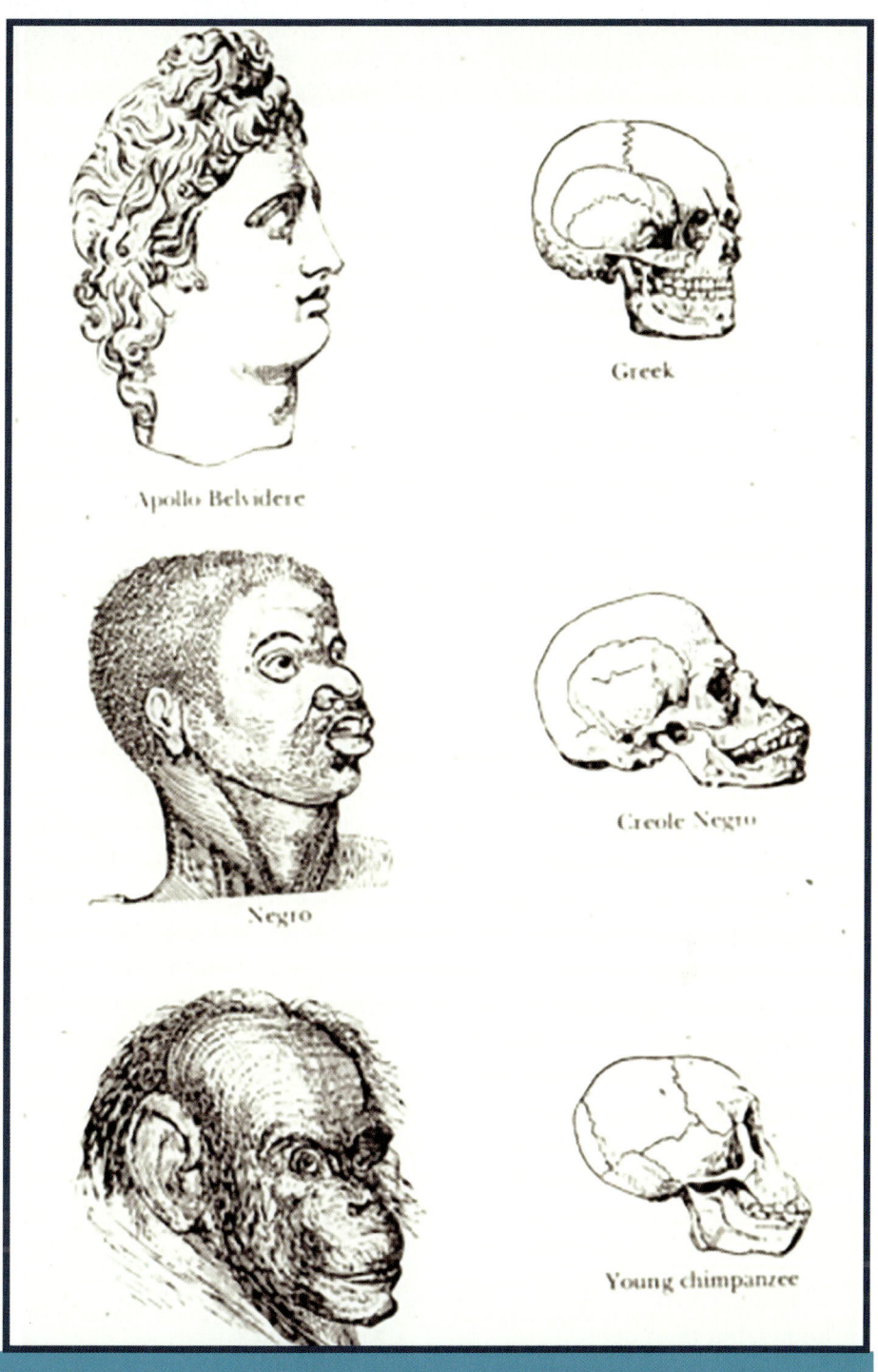

Polygenists believed there was not one human race but several. This illustration from a 1857 scientific book set out to prove that whites were as distinct from blacks as they are from chimpanzees.

VIEWS ON SLAVERY: IN THE WORDS OF ENSLAVED AFRICANS, MERCHANTS, OWNERS, AND ABOLITIONISTS

Africans and all the other people with dark skin were considered inferior to whites.

When slave trading began in the seventeenth century, white Europeans tended to view Africans as a separate kind of people. Differences in people were seen in religious terms. White people believed that God had chosen whites to lead and control the world because they were good. Many Europeans believed that since Africans were not like them and they did not believe in the same god, they could be treated like farm animals, as property.[6] Even Joseph Le Conte, who said he treated all his slaves well, wrote that the planters in his neighborhood "formed themselves into a mounted police that regularly patrolled the country by night" in order to capture and arrest slaves trying to escape. Because of this harsh control, Le Conte wrote, "There never was a more orderly, nor apparently happier, working class than the negroes of Liberty County."[7]

Even President Thomas Jefferson thought black people were inferior to whites. This founding father, who wrote the Declaration of Independence and who believed in equality and freedom, did not believe that these rights were meant for black people. Jefferson hated slavery, even though he owned more than 200 slaves. But he most hated slavery for how it affected white children. He felt it made white children very comfortable with tyranny, cruelty, and the oppression of others. Jefferson wrote in his *Notes on Virginia* about how children react when they see their parents losing their temper with a slave. "Our children see this and learn to imitate it . . . the parent storms, the child looks on . . . [and] puts on the same airs in the circle of smaller slaves, gives loose to his worst of passions and thus is nursed, educated, and daily exercised in tyranny."[8] However, Jefferson stuck to the belief that black people were childlike and lacked the intelligence of whites. In a letter to a friend, Jefferson dismissed the famous African-American poet Phillis Wheatley writing, "Misery is often the parent of the most affecting touches in poetry—Among blacks is misery enough, God knows, but not poetry."[9]

COMPLETE OBEDIENCE REQUIRED

Later in his life, Joseph Le Conte would write about why it was important that white Southerners keep black people in slavery. Le Conte saw his use of slaves as very moral and that his burden was to spend his life selflessly taking care of his slaves. In reality, Le Conte's slaves were taking care of him and his family by doing all the work on the farm. Many Southerners felt the same way as Le Conte. They saw slave ownership as a good thing, because they felt that African Americans could not take care of themselves and needed white people to guide and help them become civilized. Le Conte wrote:

> Not only has the Negro been elevated to his present condition by contact with the white race, but he is sustained in that position . . . by the same contact, and whenever that support is withdrawn he [reverts] again to his primitive state. The Negro race is still in childhood; it has not yet learned to walk alone in the paths of civilization.[10]

What went hand in hand with this belief system was a philosophy called paternalism. This was the view that Southern planters should keep order and authority on their land at all times by insisting on complete obedience from the slaves. The odd part was that slaves were supposed to feel gratitude and love for their masters in return.[11]

THE "HAPPY SLAVE" MYTH

Southern planters felt that because their slaves were dependent on them for food and shelter, they should be happy and content to serve in the fields. (The slaves were only dependent because their masters refused to allow them to provide food and shelter for themselves.) The planters made the slaves bow to them all the time. The slaves had to always stand when white people came into a room and keep standing for hours until they left. They had to endure whippings from the masters and their children.

From Joseph Le Conte's writings, we get an unflinching account of the views of many white southerners. Without question, they believed blacks were inferior beings who were happy to be slaves.

A slave could be kicked for walking between two whites on the street.[12] Slave owners also insisted that their slaves show no signs of unhappiness. Slave Henry Watson said, "The slaveholder watches every move of the slave, and if he is downcast or sad—in fact, if they are in any mood but laughing and singing . . . they are said to have the devil in them."[13]

The idea of "happy slaves" made Southerners feel better about themselves. But as the 1700s turned into the 1800s, more people started speaking out against slavery. They even started calling the slave owners evil. More Southern planters felt threatened, and they decided to defend their way of life. So the happy and contented slave became a comfortable myth that the planters clung to. People wrote books, drew pictures, and composed songs about happy slaves. Myths come in very handy when groups of people do not want to face things they are doing or have done. What shattered the myth and the Southern way of life was the American Civil War.

JOSEPH LE CONTE ON THE RUN

Joseph Le Conte describes in his autobiography how he was almost captured by the Yankees during the war. Northern Army General Sherman and his men were moving through the Georgia countryside, rounding up all the Southern men they could find. They were looking for Le Conte. He was trying to escape any way he could, and he recalled how earnestly his former slaves helped him run away.

> I paid one of my negroes twenty dollars to carry my boys back home . . . shook each heartily by the hand and bade them goodbye. 'Goodbye, Massah [master], and God bless you!' 'I hope the Lord will keep you from them Yankees, dear Massah!'—such were the parting words that greeted me . . . Were they sincere?[14]

Even Joseph Le Conte, so outwardly sure of his slaves' love for him, still had doubts. He should have doubted. The reason why his slaves were anxious to see him go was because they had taken some of Le Conte's property and were leaving with the permission of the Yankee troops. They were finally free! Frederick Douglass, the great black abolitionist, wrote that slaves stealing from their masters was moral and just: "Considering that my labor and person were the property of [my master] and that I was by him deprived of the necessaries of life—necessaries obtained by my own labor—it was easy to deduce the right to supply myself with what was my own."[15]

ACTS OF RESISTANCE

Le Conte and many other planters failed to see that slaves often wore false faces to their masters. Any group who is under the control of another group will do this for self-preservation. The oppressed group will develop code words (or songs such as "Steal Away") that their oppressors do not know, in order to communicate among themselves. They will also resist slavery in ways that create doubts in the master's mind, but do not bring on a whipping. These acts of resistance can be small, but effective. A slave might take longer to complete a task. A slave might fake confusion on how to do a job, forcing the master to do it himself. A machine might be accidentally broken or a chicken stolen for extra food for the underfed slave family. These acts of resistance gave the slaveholders the idea that slaves were mentally slow and that they liked to steal. But that is only because the slave owners could not bring themselves to believe the reality of the tyranny in which they were active participants.[16]

AFTER THE WAR

Joseph Le Conte lived to a very old age still believing in polygenism. Along with many other white Southerners, Le Conte worked very hard to deny blacks the right to vote after the Civil War. He believed that former slaves would never be as smart as whites, so only whites should rule America. Le Conte wrote about voting rights saying, "The Negro race as a whole is certainly at present . . . unworthy of the ballot. The South . . . is solid for self-government by the white race as the only self-governing race."[17]

This terrible deed was not legally undone until the Voting Rights Act in 1965 after many years of struggle. Unfortunately, some states are now trying to prevent African Americans from voting because the

> The following excerpts are from Sections 2 and 4 of the Voting Rights Act of 1965, which made voting practices, such as having to pass a literacy test before being able to vote, illegal:
>
> *SEC. 2. No voting qualification or prerequisite to voting, or standard, practice, or procedure shall be imposed or applied by any State or political subdivision to deny or abridge the right of any citizen of the United States to vote on account of race or color.*
>
> *SEC. 4. (a) To assure that the right of citizens of the United States to vote is not denied or abridged on account of race or color, no citizen shall be denied the right to vote in any Federal, State, or local election because of his failure to comply with any test or device in any State with respect to which the determinations have been made under subsection (b) or in any political subdivision with respect to which such determinations have been made as a separate unit, unless the United States District Court for the District of Columbia in an action for a declaratory judgment brought by such State or subdivision against the United States has determined that no such test or device has been used during the five years preceding the filing of the action for the purpose or with the effect of denying or abridging the right to vote on account of race or color.19*

US Supreme Court recently struck down a key provision of the Voting Rights Act that prevented racial discrimination at the polls. This court decision has allowed state legislators (who are mostly white) to pass laws that make voting difficult for people they don't want to vote.[18]

Unlike slave-owning men, who commanded absolute obedience from their slaves and family, the experience of white women under paternalism was quite different. Most Southern women willingly yielded control to their fathers and husbands. For them, the presence of slaves in the home was seen as a natural result of Southern kindness toward people less civilized. People running this way and that, doing anything a white person wanted, was the accepted order of things. Viewing slavery from this vantage point, many women felt that their relationships with their slaves were quite pleasant and caring. Lots of young ladies like Letitia Burwell were offended when Northerners put down their way of life.

CHAPTER 5

PAMPERED BLINDNESS

MANY SOUTHERN SLAVE owners were surprised and distressed that a lot of people thought of them as "dealers of human souls." They were astonished that their grand and graceful lives were seen in such harsh, unforgiving terms. After the end of the Civil War, one of them, Letitia M. Burwell, the wealthy granddaughter of a governor, decided to set the record straight. She wrote a story of her times as a young girl growing up on a Virginia plantation and her visits to other plantations in the neighboring region. Letitia felt that every single one of the slave owners she met were just and good people. She claimed to have never seen a slave abused or mistreated. She wrote that she could not believe that she was "descended from such monsters," and she wanted people to know what she felt was the

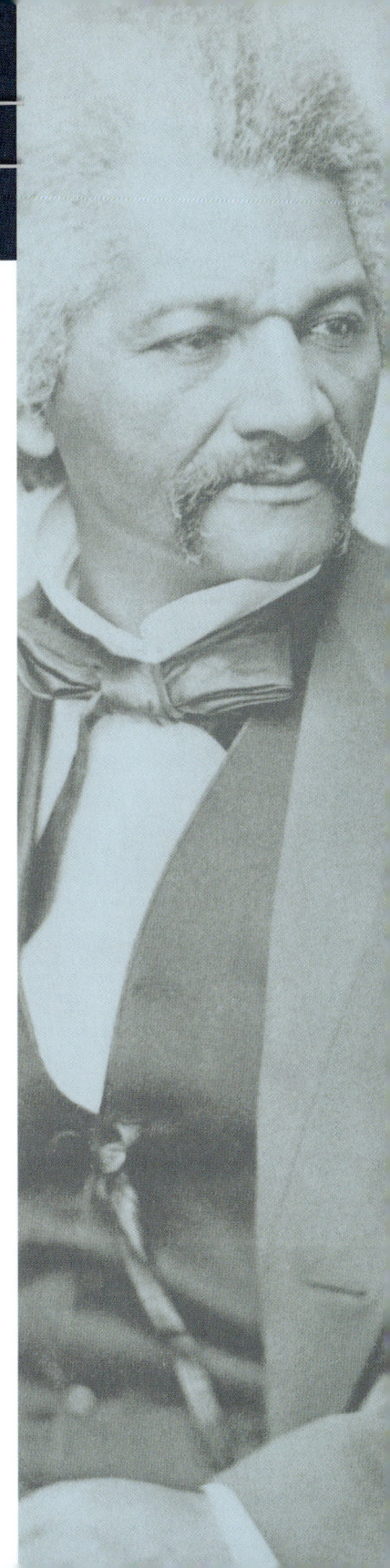

...d bless you massa! you feed
...d clothe us. When we are sick
...u nurse us, and when too old
...work, you provide for us!

These poor creatures are a sacred legacy
from my ancestors and while a dollar is
left me, nothing shall be spared to increase
their comfort and happiness.

This illustration depicts the myth of a plantation full of happy slaves. The quotes at the top reinforce the myth. Such thinking was a way for whites to justify the institution of slavery.

truth about the people who owned slaves—the "noble men and virtuous women who have passed away."[1]

LETITIA BELIEVES THE "HAPPY SLAVE" MYTH

According to Letitia, the Burwell plantation was comfortable, calm, and beautiful. Slave cabins were gaily painted white and had delicious vegetable gardens next to them. Whenever the slaves were hungry they could just pick food off the nearby trees. The male slaves sang joyfully while they worked in the fields and the women happily did their sewing, weaving, and housecleaning while their children romped and played in the yard. She wrote, "These formed the only pictures familiar to my childhood . . . all were merry-hearted, and among them I never saw a discontented [unhappy] face."[2]

SOUTHERN CULTURE AND BEING A LADY

Like most daughters of Southern plantation owners, Letitia grew up in the country and did not have much contact with big cities. She did not join women's groups or become active in political clubs like some women in the North. In Southern culture, such activities were not considered ladylike. Letitia was only taught to manage a slave household, ruled strictly by her father first, and then later, her husband. Southern women and men believed in the idea of paternalism—a white man ruling the plantation and the people on it (both black and white) with an iron hand.[3] A lady was supposed to agree with the men around her no matter what she really thought. Most important, Letitia was brought up assuming that her most common needs would be met by the everyday efforts of slaves.[4]

SLAVERY IN THE "BIG HOUSE"

Letitia Burwell called her servants "indispensables" and wrote that her family had many. Her mother chose certain slaves, at ages ten or twelve, to work in the family home, called the "Big House." Older house slaves would teach them about cleaning and cooking, everything about serving the plantation family. Burwell wrote "they might be seen constantly darting about on errands from the house to the kitchen and the cabins, upstairs and downstairs." It was common for young house slaves to sleep on bedroom floors so they could get up and serve their mistress or master in the middle of the night. Letitia really believed that the slaves enjoyed this and wrote, "These black, smiling 'indispensables' . . . insisted so good-naturedly on . . . combing [my] hair, pulling off [my] slippers—that one had not the heart to refuse."[5]

Usually older children in most families have certain chores, like taking out the trash or washing the dishes. Daughters of slaveholders did not have much of anything to do. They might take care of their own rooms a little and maybe pick some pretty flowers for decorating, but most of their time was spent visiting friends, shopping, and fixing their hair.[6] Letitia Burwell wrote, "One easily acquired a habit of being waited upon, there being so many servants with so little to do. It was natural to ask for a drink of water when the water was right at hand, and to have things brought which you might easily have gotten yourself." Letitia said the slaves were "so pleased" at serving her and her friends that she never hesitated to ask them to do the simplest things.[7]

Slaves did mostly everything for the plantation family. Many young, white girls grew up not knowing

PAMPERED BLINDNESS

Slaves provided free labor for the slave owners, even in their homes. Domestic slaves did all the cooking, cleaning, and other housework so that the plantation mistress didn't have to.

how to care for their own children, because it was assumed a slave would do it. Slave cooks prepared all the meals; so many young women never knew how to cook. House servants cleaned the house, made clothes, wove rugs, and hung drapes. Plantation girls were never taught how to do any of the things they might need to do for themselves. Interestingly, the mistress of a plantation would take credit for work she had not done herself. For example, in letters that were written at the time, some young women would complain to friends that they had been ironing clothes all day. Actually, the women had only been seeing to it that their slaves ironed the clothes.[8] Most slave-holding women never touched a hot iron or a wrinkled blouse.

BLACK WOMEN AND WHITE WOMEN

Although it was very hard to be a house slave, many mistresses and servants became strongly tied to one another. Just by seeing each other day after day, slaves and their owners sometimes became very close emotionally. Many times, the slave nurses had raised their masters and mistresses from the time they were babies. The white children grew up to love their nurses like mothers. The slaves also knew the most intimate secrets of the young, white ladies they served. Slaves needed the protection a mistress could give them from needless hardship or to escape punishment from the master. Both black women and white women were dependent on each other for certain personal freedoms, and they worked together to achieve them.[9]

Sometimes the slave and her mistress would become lifelong friends. Letitia Burwell wrote that on the Virginian

PAMPERED BLINDNESS

"ACCOMPANIED BY ONE OF THESE SMILING 'INDISPENSABLES.'"—*Page* 4.

This illustration from Letitia Burwell's book depicts the friendships that often arose between the children of plantation owners and their slaves. These could not last to adulthood, however.

Otterburn plantation, whenever the master and mistress left, they gave the keys to a particular slave to manage the place. "No more sincere attachment could have existed than that between this lady and her servant.... When the [servant] was seized with a contagious fever which ended her life, she could not have had a more faithful friend and nurse than was her mistress."[10]

AUNT FANNY STARTS A BUSINESS

House slaves could also gain much power by using their wits. These slaves got favors from their masters and mistresses because they were just better at running the plantation than their owners were. Burwell told a story of Aunt Fanny, a cook on the plantation of a famous lawyer:

> Although considered the owner of his house, it was a mistake.... This gentlemen had no 'rights' there whatever ... his house being under the entire command of Aunt Fanny ... a huge mulatto woman whose word was law and whose voice thundered abuse if any dared to disobey her.[11]

Aunt Fanny even started her own business. While cooking for the family, she would make her own popular "butter soap." One time, her owner pleaded with her to stop boiling soap because it was costing him a small fortune in firewood. And Aunt Fanny "looking at him with astonishment, but with firmness in her eye," replied, "Couldn't possibly do it ... because soap, sir, soap's my maintenance!"[12]

Aunt Fanny was a smart and enterprising person who demanded respect from her owners. The soap business was her business and she knew her particular owner would not deprive her of it because he had grown to depend on her completely. It is important to remember, though, that most slaves did not have this kind of relationship with the people who owned them. After the Civil War, the number of free black entrepreneurs actually went down in the South because whites would not purchase their goods from African-American businesses.[13]

PAMPERED BLINDNESS

> Letitita Burwell describes the death of a house slave, Aunt Fanny. Burwell does not understand or accept the slaves' religion and tries to force her own religion on Aunt Fanny while she is on her deathbed.
>
> Her room was crowded with negroes who had come to perform their religious rites around the deathbed. Joining hands, they performed a savage dance, shouting wildly around her bed. This was horrible to hear and see especially as in this family every effort had been made to instruct their negro dependents in the truths of religion; . . . But although an intelligent woman, she seemed to cling to the superstitions of her race.
>
> . . . the friend and minister of the family . . . marked some passages in the Bible, and asked me to go and read them to her. I went, and said to her: "Aunt Fanny, here are some verses Mr. Mitchell has marked for me to read to you, . . ." Then said I: "We are afraid the noise and dancing have made you worse."
>
> Speaking feebly, she replied: "Honey, dat kind o' 'ligion suit us black folks better 'an yo' kind. What suit Mars' Charles mind karn't suit mine."[14]

SOUTHERN LADIES MUST DO FOR THEMSELVES

As the Civil War raged on, many rich, young, Southern women got a small taste of what it was like to work. They had to learn many everyday tasks to support themselves and their families, such as cooking, cleaning, harvesting eggs and milk, and sewing. Still, there were many who never got over the loss of the Southern plantation style of living. Many felt that Southern slave owners had given up their freedom to devote themselves to the well-being of their slaves. Letitia Burwell wrote that all of her ancestors made sacrifices for the family's slaves. She seemed to feel that the slaves owed her and her family for helping "the naked, savage Africans to the condition of good cooks and respectable maids!"[15]

While most wealthy Southern women were being waited on hand and foot by servants, Southern black women were anxious to be free. The story of Harriet Jacobs gives another view of what life was like in the "Big House." Instead of feeling grateful, Jacobs burned with resentment. Even though paternalism limited opportunities for white women in the South, it could mean death for black women. Harriet Jacobs spent almost a lifetime running away from a cruel slave owner.

CHAPTER 6

DESPERATE TO LIVE FREE

The room was small. Built over a shed next to her grandmother's house, there was no furniture and nothing had ever lived in it except for rats and mice. The area was nine feet long and seven feet wide. It sloped down like a roof and at its tallest point the ceiling was only three feet high. There were no windows so little air or sunlight ever got in. The space was stifling, the darkness total.[1]

This is how escaped slave Harriet Jacobs would live for years. She would see the seasons change through small holes she had bored in the wood of her hiding place. Many times she would wish just once to come out and play with her two children laughing below her. She could not tell them where she was. It was too dangerous, because her owner, Dr. Flint, was searching for her, and Harriet was afraid

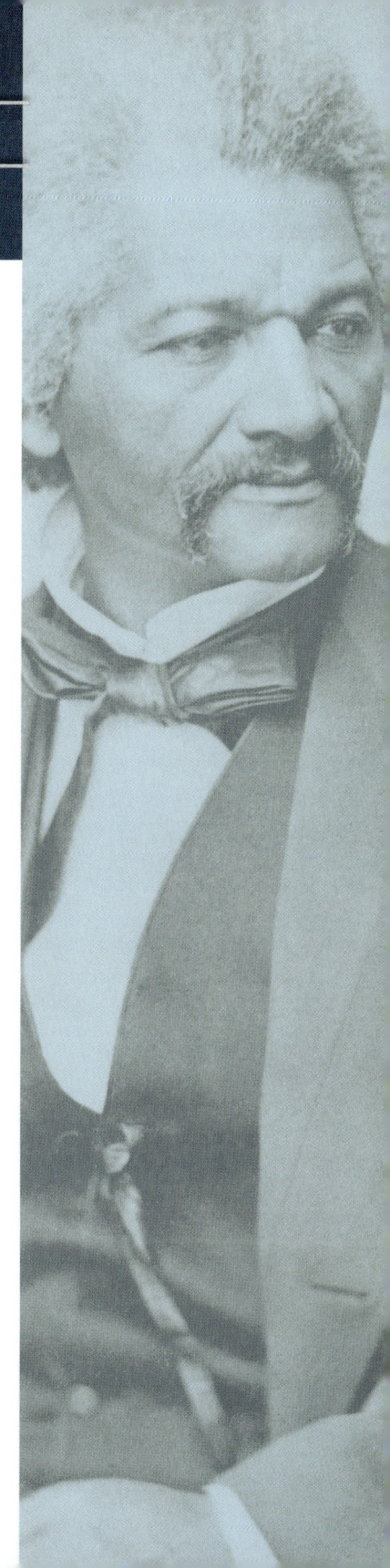

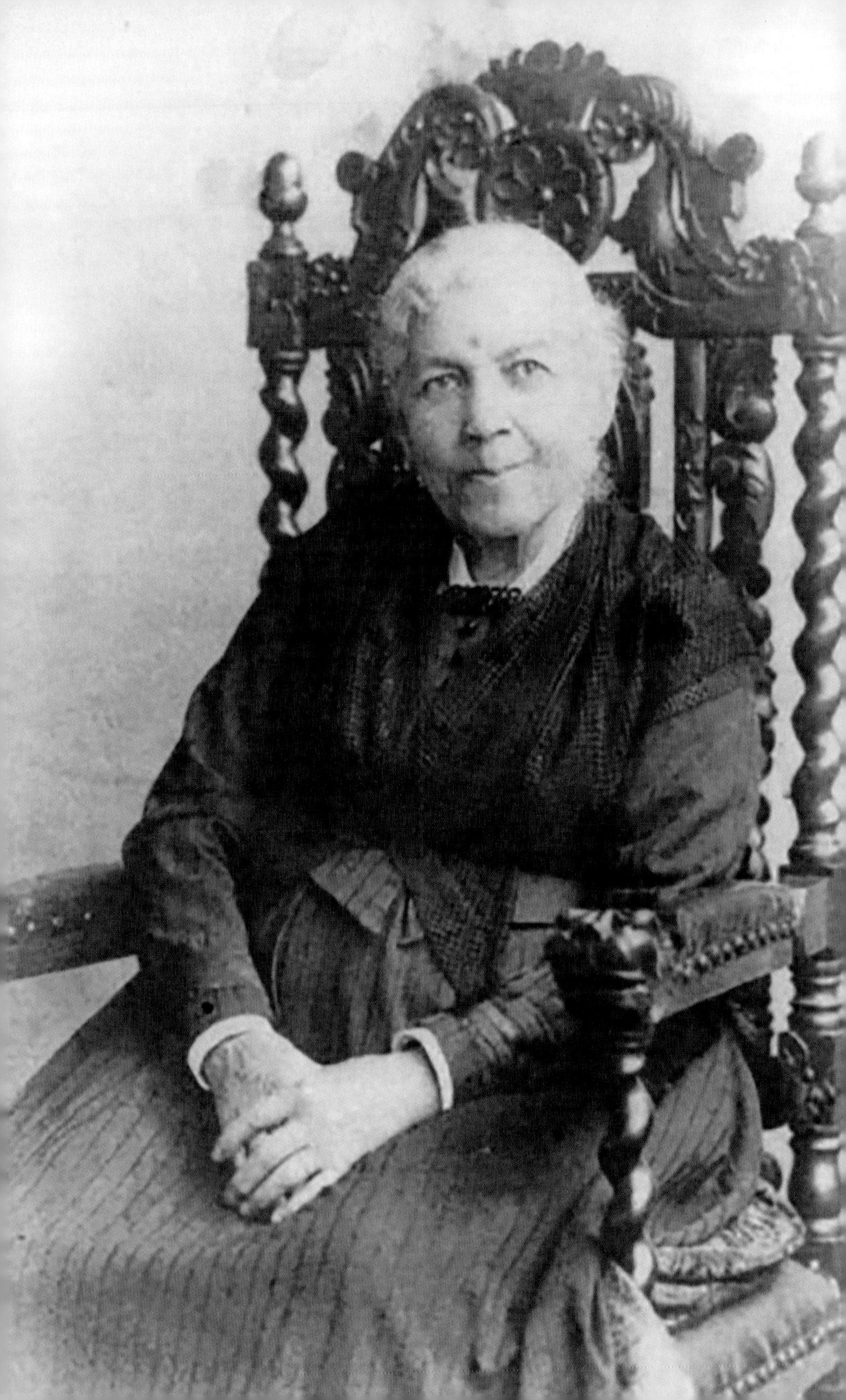

DESPERATE TO LIVE FREE

someone might see her and turn her in to the authorities. Jacobs wrote that even as hard as living in this confined room was, she "would have chosen this, rather than my lot as a slave, though white people considered it an easy one; [as] compared with the fate of others."[2]

A HAPPY CHILDHOOD

Harriet Jacobs was born into slavery in Edenton, North Carolina around 1813. She belonged to the Horniblow family, who also owned her mother and grandmother. In the South, the children of slaves were the property of the person who owned the mother, not the father.[3] By the time Harriet was a small girl, her grandmother had bought her own freedom with the money she had made baking crackers late at night after she had gotten all of her work done during the day. Her grandmother had hoped someday to buy the rest of her family.[4] It was not to be.

In her autobiography, Jacobs described a happy childhood and how she did not even know she was a slave until she was six years old. She found out when her mother died suddenly. She learned from people whispering around her that she belonged to her dead mother's mistress. Luckily for Harriet, this mistress had been a good friend to Harriet's mother. She taught Harriet to read and write. This was a rare thing since it was illegal to educate a slave. The mistress did not ask Harriet to work day and night like other slave owners. Harriet would write of those days, "I would sit by her

---

Harriet Jacobs escaped slavery and went on to write a memoir describing the harsh treatment and sexual abuse she endured as a slave. Jacobs was a popular abolitionist speaker and a social reformer.

side for hours, sewing diligently, with a heart as free from care as that of any free-born white child. . . . Those were happy days—too happy to last."[5]

HARRIET'S MISTRESS DIES

When Harriet was almost twelve years old, her mistress died. Jacobs had loved her very much and was hoping that her mistress had written in her will that, upon her death, Harriet would be freed. Harriet's friends were confident that she would be freed. However, when the will was read, Harriet discovered that her mistress had given her to her five-year-old niece. Harriet was devastated. She remembered how her mistress had taught her a Bible verse—"*Thou shalt love thy neighbor as thyself.*" Harriet took that sentiment to heart upon learning it. "But I was her slave, and I suppose she did not recognize me as her neighbor."[6]

LONELY AND FEARFUL

Harriet soon was taken to the home of Dr. Flint to be slave to his little daughter, Emily. (Dr. Flint is the name Jacobs used in her memoirs. His real name was James Norcom.) When she arrived at her new home she encountered "cold looks, cold words, and cold treatment. . . . On my narrow bed I moaned and wept, I felt so desolate and alone."[7]

In a few days, Harriet realized that Mrs. Flint was nothing like her first mistress. Instead of being filled with gentleness, Mrs. Flint had "nerves . . . so strong, that she could sit in her easy chair and see a woman whipped, till the blood trickled from every stroke of the lash."[8] If Sunday dinner was not served exactly on time, Mrs. Flint would wait until all the food had been dished out to her guests and then spit in "all the kettles and pans that had been used for cooking."[9] She would do this so the slaves would not want to eat the usual leftovers, sometimes the only food offered to the slaves.

DR. FLINT'S ABUSE

When Harriet turned fifteen years old, things began to change drastically for the worse. This time it was not Mrs. Flint's torment Harriet feared, but Dr. Flint's. He started to speak "foul words" to her. He began to ask her to touch places on his body that Harriet's grandmother had told her not to touch until she was married to someone she loved. Dr. Flint demanded to touch her in her private places, too. Disgusted and frightened, Harriet avoided him as much as possible. But he was her owner, "I was compelled to live under the same roof with him—where I saw a man of forty years my senior daily violating the most sacred commandments of nature. He told me I was his property; that I must be subject to his will in all things."[10]

Black slave women experienced life much differently on the plantations than white women. Under paternalism, husbands or fathers governed the white women. These same white men ruled female slaves, too.[11] Black fathers and husbands had little say in how their wives and daughters were treated. Many times, they had to sit by and watch as the white slave owner took advantage of their loved ones. Some men struck back to defend their loved ones, but it was dangerous and could lead to death.

HARRIET RUNS AWAY

Harriet had to take her fate into her own hands. She sought protection from a local white man, Mr. Sands. Over time, she had two beautiful children with him. But even as the years passed, Dr. Flint did not stop pursuing Harriet Jacobs relentlessly. He threatened to send her and her children to work in the hot sun on his plantation rather than work in the coolness of his house. He threatened to sell her children to punish her for running away from him. He beat her. Jacobs was frantic. She disappeared from sight and hid in a spare room of a good friend of her family, a white woman who owned slaves.[12] She thought that Dr. Flint would forget about her after awhile. But he never did.

FLINT IS TRICKED

Dr. Flint thought Jacobs had fled to New York and went to look for her there. He put advertisements in the paper offering money to anyone who would capture her if they saw her. He put Jacobs's brother William and her two children in jail, hoping that she would come out of hiding to help them. His obsession had gotten the better of him and he was in need of money to keep up the search for her.[13] A slave trader, who wanted to buy Harriet Jacobs's two children and their uncle, approached him. Dr. Flint said, "I have been reflecting upon your proposition and I have concluded to let you have the three negroes if you will pay nineteen hundred dollars."[14] Dr. Flint did not know that this particular slave trader was an agent of the children's father, Mr. Sands. In a great stroke of luck and cunning, Dr. Flint had been tricked into selling Jacobs's children to their own father. The children would be free.

When Dr. Flint found out about this brave deception, he was furious. He went to Jacobs's grandmother and said, "I shall soon have her. You need never expect to see her free. She shall be my slave as long as I live, and when I am dead she shall be the slave of my children."[15] Dr. Flint left. But Jacobs rejoiced. Her children were finally free, even if she herself was not. She wrote, "Whatever slavery might do to me, it could not shackle my children . . . my little ones were saved."[16]

DESPERATE TO LIVE FREE

Like Harriet Jacobs, many slaves were helped by white abolitionists, who hid them on their property until they felt it was safe to move on.

VIEWS ON SLAVERY: IN THE WORDS OF ENSLAVED AFRICANS, MERCHANTS, OWNERS, AND ABOLITIONISTS

ESCAPING THROUGH SNAKY SWAMP

Unfortunately, a curious slave who kept jiggling the doorknob of the secret room came across Jacobs' hiding place. She had to get out before she was discovered, so the woman brought Jacobs a disguise. It was a sailor's outfit with a jacket and pants.[17] Jacobs could not thank her enough, but her friend kissed her on the cheek and just told her to practice walking like a sailor with her hands in her pockets. If Jacobs were discovered, they both would be in danger. It was against the law for anyone to hide escaped slaves.

Jacobs was helped onto a nearby boat by friends and then stayed in a local bog waiting for her uncle to prepare a hiding place for her. After a horrid night of snakes and mosquitoes, Jacobs was rowed ashore and walked to her grandmother's house wearing her sailor's clothes. She even passed the father of her children on the street, but he had no idea who she was. Her friend said, "You must make the most of this walk . . . for you may not have another very soon." Jacobs thought his voice sounded sad. Later she would write, "It was kind of him to conceal from me what a dismal hole was to be my home for a long, long time."[18]

A TINY ROOM TO HIDE IN

Harriet Jacobs would be in that tiny room over her grandmother's shed for seven years. Her Uncle Phillip and Aunt Nancy would pass food up to her through a trap door. Sometimes they would come up to talk to her at night. Jacobs could not stand in an erect position, so she crawled around the small area for exercise. Harriet found a way to bore holes in the wood so she could get more fresh air. She wrote, "I sat by it till late into the night, to enjoy the little whiff of air that floated in." She watched her children through those holes too. "At last I heard the merry laugh of children, and presently two sweet little faces were looking up at me, as though they knew I was there, and were conscious of the joy they imparted. How I longed to tell them I was there!"[19]

DESPERATE TO LIVE FREE

$50 REWARD.

Ranaway from the subscriber on TUESDAY MORNING, 26th ULTIMO, My negro boy calling himself Severn Black. The said negro is about 5 feet six inches in height, chesnut color, has a scar on his upper lip, downcast countenance when spoken to, blink-eyed, showing a great deal of white, long bushy hair, is about twenty years old, had on when he left a blue fustian Jacket, pantaloons of a greyish color, blue striped shirt, A BLACK SLOUCH HAT and shoes nearly worn out.

The above reward will be paid by me for the apprehension and delivery of the said negro in the County Jail at Princess Anne, Somerset county, Maryland. April 1, 1861. RICHARD E. SNELLING.

SOMERSET HERALD Print, Princess Anne, Md.

This newspaper advertisement from the April 1, 1861, edition of the Princess Anne, Maryland, *Somerset Herald* offers a reward for the return of an escaped slave to his oppressors.

ESCAPE TO PHILADELPHIA!

After many years of agonizing confinement, Harriet Jacobs was finally smuggled on board a boat sailing north to Philadelphia, Pennsylvania. The boat passed the Snaky Swamp and Jacobs remembered the horrible night spent there. She shuddered at the thought of the bugs and crawly things in there, but the cool evening air calmed her from thoughts of the past. As the night wore on, Jacobs could not sleep. She was too excited. Could this be really happening to her? She was on deck at the crack of dawn and for the first time in her life she saw the sun rise on free soil. She watched the sky redden, and it seemed like the familiar ball of flame rose slowly and majestically out of the ocean. It made the waves sparkle "and everything caught the beautiful glow." She stood on the deck with another escaped slave named Fanny, and they put their arms around each other, lost in the beauty of the day.

> Before us lay the city of strangers. We looked at each other, and [our] eyes . . . were moistened with tears. We had escaped from slavery, and we supposed ourselves to be safe from the hunters. But we were alone in the world, and we had left dear ties behind us.[20]

FINALLY FREE

In Philadelphia, the Anti-Slavery Society, a Quaker group devoted to aiding runaway slaves from the South, helped Harriet Jacobs find a job and place to stay. Even though she had made it to the North, this did not mean she was safe. Legislation passed by the United States Congress in 1850 commanded "all good citizens" who knew of escaped slaves living in the North to notify the authorities so that they could be captured and taken back down South again. It was called the Fugitive Slave Act.[21] With Dr. Flint still in pursuit, Jacobs would never feel out of harm's way. Any day, she could be ripped from the freedom of the

This graphic was printed on the side of collection boxes for the Massachusetts Antislavery Society. It encouraged people to display the boxes in their homes to collect contributions from visitors.

North. Even though Jacobs was reunited with her two children, she herself was still owned by the Flint family. It was not until years later, after Dr. Flint died, that one of Jacobs's abolitionist friends would buy her freedom from the husband of a now grown-up Emily Flint, Harriet's old mistress.[22]

> Harriet Jacobs described how religious leaders from the North were often fooled by Southern slaveholders:
>
>   *A clergyman who goes to the south, for the first time, has usually some feeling . . . that slavery is wrong. The slaveholder suspects this, and plays his game accordingly. He makes himself as agreeable as possible; . . . After dinner [the clergyman] walks round the premises, and sees the . . . comfortable huts of favored household slaves. . . . He asks [the slaves] if they want to be free, and they say, "O, no, massa." This is sufficient to satisfy him. He comes home . . . [and] assures people that he has been to the south, and seen slavery for himself; . . . that the slaves don't want their freedom; that they have hallelujah meetings, and other religious privileges.*
>
>   *What does he know of the half-starved wretches toiling from dawn till dark on the plantations? of mothers shrieking for their children, torn from their arms by slave traders? of young girls dragged down into moral filth? of pools of blood around the whipping post? of hounds trained to tear human flesh? of men screwed into cotton gins to die? The slaveholder showed him none of these things, and the slaves dared not tell of them if he had asked them.*[23]

BECOMING AN ABOLITIONIST

Harriet Jacobs joined the abolitionists and traveled extensively with her Quaker friend Amy Post, a white lady. They both spoke against slavery and Post urged Jacobs to write her life story. The experience of writing brought back painful memories, so Harriet distanced herself from the tale. She used a fictitious name, "Linda Brent," because she was embarrassed by some of the things she had done in her life. However, slavery forced many people to make choices they never would have made on their own in a free and just society. Desperate times often call for desperate measures. Harriet Jacobs was no different. So she gathered her courage and set down her journey to freedom on paper. She has left behind, for the world to appreciate, an unbelievable and amazing account of one woman's survival and personal strength.

When Jacobs reached Philadelphia, she discovered a whole support network devoted to runaway slaves who wanted to make new lives for themselves. Two men were very influential in that network—William Lloyd Garrison, a white man, and Frederick Douglass, an African American. The publication of Garrison's newspaper *The Liberator* would mark the beginning of the abolitionist movement. Douglass would inspire generations after him to seek justice and freedom for all.

CHAPTER 7

FREEDOM'S HEROES

So profoundly ignorant of the nature of slavery are many persons, that they are stubbornly incredulous whenever they read or listen to any recital of the cruelties which are daily inflicted on its victims. They do not deny that the slaves are held as property; but that terrible fact seems to convey to their minds no idea of injustice, exposure to outrage, or savage barbarity.
—*Frederick Douglass* [1]

On this subject [slavery], I do not wish to think, or speak, or write, with moderation. No! no! . . . I am in earnest—I will not equivocate—I will not excuse—I will not retreat a single inch—AND I WILL BE HEARD.
—*William Lloyd Garrison* [2]

Two men challenged the nation to explain how the American people justified to themselves that some fellow citizens were legally being bought and sold like livestock. Freedom, the most basic value and individual right, was being regularly denied to many people in the United States. One of these men was a former slave. His name was Frederick Douglass. The other man was William Lloyd Garrison, the son of a merchant seaman from Massachusetts.

TWO LIVES THAT SOUGHT FREEDOM

Douglass had grown up owned by the Auld family. Sophie Auld, his owner's wife, had begun to teach him to read, but her husband threatened her and put a stop to it immediately. From then on, Douglass figured that if whites were that afraid of slaves reading and writing, he would teach himself. He carried a Webster's pocket spelling book with him wherever he went and learned from the white boys he played with on the Baltimore streets.[3]

Garrison's father deserted him and his family, and young William was forced to work selling homemade molasses candy and firewood. As a young man, he apprenticed on a newspaper as a writer and editor. Later he published and edited this country's most influential abolitionist newspaper—*The Liberator*.[4]

These individuals were two of the most influential abolitionist figures in the United States in the decades leading up to the Civil War. They believed in freedom for the slaves, but they disagreed on how to go about making that happen. Each man had a strong will and a fierce intelligence. They would change a nation.

DOUGLASS BECOMES FAMOUS

Douglass was a star-struck young man, newly escaped to the North. He had disguised himself and, with the help of a friend's fake identification papers, hopped on a train out of Baltimore.[5] He became familiar with Garrison's paper, *The Liberator*, and it changed his life. "*The Liberator*

An illustration of Frederick Douglass's escape from slavery was used on the cover of the sheet music to the 1845 composition "The Fugitive's Song," written by the abolitionist Jesse Hutchinson.

was a paper after my own heart. It detested slavery.... I not only liked—I *loved* this paper, and its editor. He seemed a match for all the opponents of emancipation.... Every week *The Liberator* came, and every week I made myself master of its contents."[6]

It was not long before Frederick Douglass was speaking before large antislavery crowds in New England. "Young . . . and hopeful, I entered upon this new life in the full gush of unsuspecting enthusiasm. The cause was good; the men engaged in it were good; the means to attain its triumph, good. . . . Freedom must soon be given to the

> In *Narrative of the Life of Frederick Douglass, an American Slave*, Douglass describes the reasons why slaves often said they were happy when asked:
>
> ... slaves, when inquired of as to their condition and the character of their masters, almost universally say they are contented, and that their masters are kind. The slaveholders have been known to send in spies among their slaves, to ascertain their views and feelings in regard to their condition. The frequency of this has had the effect to establish among the slaves the maxim, that a still tongue makes a wise head. They suppress the truth rather than take the consequences of telling it, and in so doing prove themselves a part of the human family. If they have any thing to say of their masters, it is generally in their masters' favor, especially when speaking to an untried man. I have been frequently asked, when a slave, if I had a kind master, and do not remember ever to have given a negative answer; nor did I, in pursuing this course, consider myself as uttering what was absolutely false; for I always measured the kindness of my master by the standard of kindness set up among slaveholders around us.[7]

Escaped slave and influential abolitionist Frederick Douglass believed that white abolitionists needed to hear about the atrocities of slavery in order to act quickly.

pining millions under ruthless bondage."[8] Week after week, Frederick Douglass would stand and speak to the people. In 1846, he told an audience: "This is American slavery: No education . . . forbidden by law to learn to read! If a mother shall teach her children to read, the law in Louisiana proclaims that she may be hanged by the neck. . . . Three millions of people shut out from the light of knowledge!"[9]

He was made to show the scars on his back from the repeated whippings he endured from a brutal overseer when he was a teenager. The people groaned at the scars and winced at his tales, but Frederick Douglass sensed something was wrong. He felt he was a curiosity, someone to be stared at rather than to be taken seriously. Douglass knew that being a fugitive slave lecturer was something important, but it was not enough for him to "narrate wrongs." He wanted to "*denounce* them."[10]

GARRISON PUBLISHES A NEWSPAPER

The first issue of Garrison's *Liberator* appeared in January 1831. It was the result of an antislavery movement that had been building for a long time. The argument put forth by the New England Anti-Slavery Society (led by Garrison) had five main points:

- Slavery was against the teachings of Christianity and the universal brotherhood of man.
- Slavery contradicted the fundamental principle of American life: freedom as an individual right.
- Slavery was economically unwise since it depended on enforced labor and lacked efficiency.
- The culture of the United States suffered because the master-slave relationship brought out the worst aspects of people. Random power over another tends to intoxicate and corrupt the people in power and the entire society.
- Slavery was a threat to the peace of the country since the South was arming itself because of a widespread fear of a slave uprising.[11]

In the first issue of his abolitionist newspaper, *The Liberator*, William Lloyd Garrison stated, "I shall strenuously contend for the immediate enfranchisement of our slave population."

Frederick Douglass agreed with all these points. By the 1850s, though, he strongly disagreed with Garrison's idea of how to end slavery. Garrison and many abolitionists believed wholeheartedly in moral persuasion. He felt that the only way to get Southern slave owners to free their slaves was to convince them that slavery was a sin against God. Garrison felt that the Constitution of the United States was a document that condoned slavery and, for this reason, the Union did not need to be preserved because the whole country was founded on injustice. In a speech, Garrison said, "Give us Disunion with liberty and a good conscience, rather than Union with slavery and moral degradation . . . shall we shake hands with those who buy, sell, torture, and . . . trade in human flesh! God forbid!"[12]

That the North should hold "no union with slaveholders," was Garrison's principle, meaning he was not about to cooperate with Southerners. He believed you had to change people before you changed government, and his opinion was one of "non-resistance."[13] Garrison did not think that the abolitionist movement should be involved in politics and that moral purity was more important than political give and take. The South was to be shunned, in Garrison's view, until they came around to the right and moral way of thinking.[14]

DOUGLASS BELIEVES IN THE CONSTITUTION

When Congress passed the Fugitive Slave Act in 1850, many black abolitionists felt that Garrison's approach was unrealistic. Douglass felt that many white abolitionists did not understand the day-to-day reality of being a slave. People were suffering. And there needed to be action. Too many people were hurting and being denied justice. Waiting for a total change in the Southern viewpoint was not practical at all. Maybe Garrison could wait around for years, but Douglass could not.

Frederick Douglass began to see that voting was "a legitimate and powerful means of abolishing slavery." Unlike Garrison, he thought that the Constitution was an antislavery document, which demanded the end of slavery "as a condition of its own existence."[15] Douglass was shocked by "the sentiment of the leader of the disunion forces [Garrison] . . . that if one vote of his would emancipate every slave in this country, he would not cast that vote."[16] He was convinced that the Constitution evoked the supreme law of the land: "to form a more perfect union, establish justice, insure domestic tranquility, provide for the common defense, promote the general welfare and secure the blessings of liberty."[17] So Douglass broke with his friend William Lloyd Garrison and the two friends never reconciled. Douglass started his own newspaper, the *North Star*, to put forth his views. It was named after the star that led slaves North to freedom on the Underground Railroad.

ABOLITIONISTS SPLIT INTO FACTIONS

Six years before the start of the Civil War, Douglass wrote an essay describing "Three Kinds of Abolitionists." In it, he outlined his feelings about the state of the antislavery movement. He saw the differences among the Republican Party (at this time the Republican Party was brand new), Garrisonian Abolitionists, and Radical Abolitionists.[18]

The Republican Party was also called the Free Soil Party, because they believed that slavery should not be extended outside the South. Its motto was "No Slavery Outside the Slave States." It is important to remember that the United States was quickly establishing new territories, and the Republicans wanted to prevent slavery from becoming a part of life there. They figured that slavery in the South would eventually end, "for lack of room and air in which to breathe."[19]

The Garrisonian Abolitionists were opposed to any political action against slavery. This included not voting. Douglass wrote: "They are in

An Address

To the PUBLIC,

FROM THE

Pennsylvania Society for promoting the Abolition of Slavery, and the Relief of Free Negroes, unlawfully held in Bondage.

*I*T is with peculiar satisfaction we assure the friends of humanity, that in prosecuting the design of our association, our endeavours have proved successful, far beyond our most sanguine expectations.

Encouraged by this success, and by the daily progress of that luminous and benign spirit of liberty, which is diffusing itself throughout the world; and humbly hoping for the continuance of the divine blessing on our labors, we have ventured to make an important addition to our original plan, and do therefore, earnestly solicit the support and assistance, of all who can feel the tender emotions of sympathy and compassion, or relish the exalted pleasure of beneficence.

Slavery is such an atrocious debasement of human nature, that its very extirpation, if not performed with solicitous care, may sometimes open a source of serious evils.

The unhappy man who has long been treated as a brute animal, too frequently sinks beneath the common standard of the human species. The galling chains that bind his body, do also fetter his intellectual faculties, and impair the social affections of his heart. Accustomed to move like a mere machine, by the will of a master, reflection is suspended; he has not the power of choice; and reason and conscience, have but little influence over his conduct: because he is chiefly governed by the passion of fear. He is poor and friendless—perhaps worn out by extreme labor, age and disease.

Under such circumstances, freedom may often prove a misfortune to himself, and prejudicial to society.

Attention to emancipated black people, it is therefore to be hoped, will become a branch of our national police; but as far as we contribute to promote this emancipation, so far that attention is evidently a serious duty, incumbent on us, and which we mean to discharge to the best of our judgment and abilities.

To instruct; to advise; to qualify those who have been restored to freedom, for the exercise and enjoyment of civil liberty. To promote in them habits of industry; to furnish them with employments suited to their age, sex, talents, and other circumstances; and to procure their children an education calculated for their future situation in life. These are the great outlines of the annexed plan, which we have adopted, and which we conceive will essentially promote the public good, and the happiness of these our hitherto too much neglected fellow creatures.

A Plan so extensive cannot be carried into execution, without considerable pecuniary resources, beyond the present ordinary funds of the society. We hope much from the generosity of enlightened and benevolent freemen, and will gratefully receive any donations or subscriptions for this purpose, which may be made to our treasurer, James Starr, or to James Pemberton, chairman, of our committee of correspondence.

Signed by order of the Society,

B. FRANKLIN, *President.*

Philadelphia, 9th of *November*, 1789.

Divisions had occurred within the abolitionist movement since the time Benjamin Franklin wrote this antislavery address, as Frederick Douglass suggested in his essay, "Three Kinds of Abolitionists."

VIEWS ON SLAVERY: IN THE WORDS OF ENSLAVED AFRICANS, MERCHANTS, OWNERS, AND ABOLITIONISTS

the country, but at the same time, they profess to stand outside of the Government." Frederick Douglass felt that the Garrisons were telling slaves to fend for themselves and quoted something Garrison had written, "All the slave asks of us, is to stand out of the way . . . God will vindicate the oppressed, by the laws of justice which he has founded.

The Liberator was a platform for abolitionists to speak their minds on slavery. Garrison ran the newspaper for 34 years.

... Stand alone, and let no cement of the Union bind the slave and he will right himself."[20] Defiantly, Douglass responded, "The idea of a slave righting himself, presupposes his ability to do so, unaided by Northern interference. O no! the slave *cannot* 'right himself' any more than an infant can grapple with a giant."[21]

The Radical Abolitionists, who had broken with the Garrison group, formed their own political party— the Liberty Party. This was the organization Douglass joined. The Liberty party believed *all* slavery was illegal because the Constitution guaranteed the blessings of liberty to *all* people. One could not wait until Southerners saw their moral error. One could not allow the Southern states to keep their slaves while denying new states that right. Slavery had to go. All of it. Douglass felt Radical Abolitionism took an ax to the root of the slavery tree. One had to "tear it up root and branch," and the only way this could be done was to keep the Union intact and push the federal government to abolish all slavery. Douglass thought Garrison was wrong. Ignoring the slave states was not an option. "By withdrawing from the Slave States, we withdraw from nearly four million Abolitionists, black and white."[22]

SOUTHERN SLAVE-OWNERS HARDEN

As the abolitionist debate heated up, the Southern position regarding slavery hardened. They were digging in. The easiest way to keep curious fellow citizens from questioning the popular attitudes of their neighbors was censorship and silence.

At first, few whites in the country talked about slavery. People were afraid of what debate would bring. A lot of Northerners had made their family fortunes in the slave trade. Southerners had built their comfortable lifestyle on the unpaid work of slaves. When abolitionists *did* begin to talk about slavery, angry mobs would break up their meetings. People giving out antislavery newspapers were beaten in town squares. Printing presses that put out antislavery essays were destroyed. Elijah Lovejoy, an editor from Illinois, was murdered by a group of people while he was trying to protect his printing press.[23] In 1835, a former governor of South Carolina led a takeover of a post office and destroyed bags of antislavery mail. In fact, from 1835 until the Civil War, there was an unofficial policy agreed to by the postmasters general of the United States that abolitionist writing was to be kept out of the mail system.[24] Garrison even wrote in *The Liberator* about bias in the press:

> . . . for a quarter of a century abolitionism . . . has been lampooned . . . vilified, unceasingly and universally, by the journals of the day . . . its advocates have been held up as crazy fanatics . . . and its meetings represented as unworthy of countenance by sane and decent men! [25]

EVEN ABOLITIONISTS WERE PREJUDICED

Printing presses being burned? Mail not being delivered? People being whipped for merely speaking their minds? But Frederick Douglass knew how deep racial prejudice went. He wrote about his white abolitionist friends in New England who struggled with their deep-rooted feelings:

> I found this prejudice very strong. . . . When it was said to me, "Mr. Douglass, I will walk to meeting with you; I am not afraid of a black man," I could not help thinking—seeing nothing very frightful in my appearance—"and why should you be?" The children of the north had all been educated to believe that if they were bad, the old *black* man—not the old *devil*—would get them. . . . [26]

TWO HEROES FIGHTING ON

Even though both men disagreed about how to end slavery, they never gave up. After each setback in the law, they counterpunched with an answering opinion. When President Lincoln announced the Emancipation Proclamation in 1863, Douglass wrote, "I never saw enthusiasm before. Men, women, young and old, were up. Hats and bonnets were in the air and we gave three cheers for Abraham Lincoln and three cheers for almost everybody else." [27] Garrison wrote in the final issue of *The Liberator* that it is, "Better to be always in a minority of one . . . branded as a madman . . . fanatic . . . frowned upon by 'the powers that be,' and mobbed by the populace . . . in defense of the right."[28]

It was not to last. The first Civil Rights legislation passed by Congress in 1875, which declared that all citizens were equal and entitled to all privileges under the law, was judged to be unconstitutional by the Supreme Court of the United States in 1883. It would not be until the 1960s that the law would grant full civil rights to the great-grandchildren of slaves.

CHAPTER 8

"WE ARE THE CHANGE THAT WE SEEK"

All these stories provide a glimpse into how actual people viewed slavery in America. Depending on their particular experiences, each person confidently believed certain ideas, and misjudged others because of it. Each story was told from an individual perspective shaped by distinctive understandings of the world around them. Some of these people lived and died never changing their minds about American slavery. Yet others, like John Newton and Frederick Douglass, moved beyond their assumptions and lived up to what President Barack Obama would say more than one hundred years later: that "We are the change that we seek."[1]

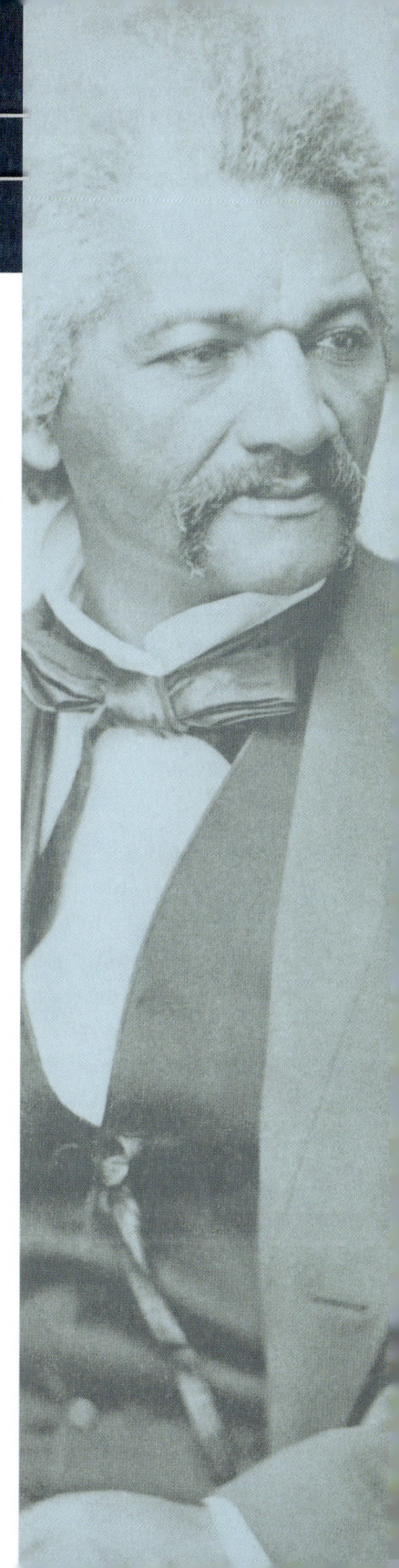

VIEWS ON SLAVERY: IN THE WORDS OF ENSLAVED AFRICANS, MERCHANTS, OWNERS, AND ABOLITIONISTS

THE SLAVE TRADER

John Newton was astonished at his own blindness to the injustices of slavery while he was the captain of a slave trading ship. He never gave a thought that what he was doing might be wrong. In Newton's time, many white people believed that if someone did not worship Jesus, then that person was an ignorant savage. Also, people with dark skin were seen as bad because they represented wickedness in the religion of the Europeans. White people believed they were good because white represented righteousness and purity in their faith. Africans worshipped their own gods and thrived within their own unique cultures, but many white people did not understand these cultures. They did not comprehend that another way of life might be as vital as their own.

THE SLAVES

Olaudah Equiano was happy living in his village in the Kingdom of Benin. Olaudah never gave a thought that someday he might be kidnapped and taken across the ocean, far from his family. He had never seen white men before and, at first, believed they would eat him. They put him in a hot and stifling ship's hold with sick and terrified people. Olaudah had no knowledge of the South or the money that was made from the slave trade. He was not used to the utter cruelty that was perpetrated against him and the others on the ship with him. But like Henry Bibb, Equiano felt that it was wrong for one person to own another. The reason why Equiano and Bibb could feel this way was because they perceived whites and blacks as equally human. Many whites did not.

    New scholarship has emerged that questions the truthfulness of Equiano's birth in Africa, and it claims that he was actually born in South Carolina. It has caused quite a controversy.[2] However, any autobiography tends to be written from the perceptions and desires of the writer and is not always factual. Equiano was supremely interested in ending slavery, so he wanted his book to be as persuasive as possible to British and American audiences. It remains a very powerful book.[3]

Harriet Jacobs fled from slavery because of the extreme abuse she was forced to endure. Many slaves like her refused the continued torment and ran away. Jacobs not only had the courage to escape and save her family, but also sincerely told her story to others even though it was painful for her.

THE SCIENTIFIC RACIST

Scientist and slave owner Joseph Le Conte wholeheartedly believed that people who had dark skin were inferior to those with white skin. Le Conte was a supporter of polygenism, a conviction that physical differences in people were directly connected to their intelligence and that these differences made some people inferior. Later, this idea would be considered racism. This "scientific" thinking became the reason why it was a good thing for slavery to continue.

To people like Le Conte, black slaves were too childlike, unskilled, and unintelligent to take care of themselves. Many whites felt that slavery was a wise thing because it taught blacks how to be "civilized." In reality, most whites could not openly admit to themselves that they were the dependent ones. The entire Southern civilization had been built on the enslavement of African-American labor.

THE SOUTHERN DAUGHTER

Letitia Burwell's story of her life as a daughter of a wealthy plantation owner was another side of white dependency on black slave labor. A young girl growing up under paternalism could not see that her society was walking a fine edge between the myth of the happy slave and the unspoken fears of slave revolt. Either slaves loved their masters or they did not. It seems strange that Southern slave owners could believe both things at the same time, but they did. While Southerners loved to glorify the sweetness of slaves contentedly singing in the fields, they

VIEWS ON SLAVERY: IN THE WORDS OF ENSLAVED AFRICANS, MERCHANTS, OWNERS, AND ABOLITIONISTS

After slavery was formally abolished in the United States, racist whites found other ways to oppress blacks. The Ku Klux Klan terrorized blacks mercilessly for decades.

also hid their deepest fears of angry slaves wanting to take revenge against their captors. Within their own hearts, many slave owners believed that it was wrong to own another person, just like Henry Bibb and Olaudah Equiano. But they had too much at stake to admit it to themselves. To confess their error meant they would have to renounce generations of Southern tradition. They could not do it.

THE ABOLITIONISTS

William Lloyd Garrison and Frederick Douglass differed in their approaches, but not in their ultimate goal: to end slavery. Garrison led the charge of the abolitionist movement, while Douglass helped carry it all the way to the Civil War. Even after the war had started, Douglass helped convince President Abraham Lincoln that African Americans should be allowed to fight against the South.

SLAVERY ENDS, BUT NOT THE HATE

After the Civil War forcibly ended slavery, it did not mean that attitudes had changed. White Americans held to their mistaken beliefs and fears and devised other means to oppress blacks since owning another human being was now against the law. In 1865, a terrorist organization called the Ku Klux Klan (KKK) was formed. These terrorists had the enthusiastic backing of former slave owners. Its creed demanded "a white man's government in this country," and the group professed to promote "Chivalry, Humanity,

VIEWS ON SLAVERY: IN THE WORDS OF ENSLAVED AFRICANS, MERCHANTS, OWNERS, AND ABOLITIONISTS

The Black Lives Matter movement was formed in response to what many people believe is institutional racism on the part of police forces across the United States.

"WE ARE THE CHANGE THAT WE SEEK"

Mercy, and Patriotism."[4] Membership in this group became widespread as planters and poor whites joined forces and donned white robes to terrorize African Americans by burning down their homes, stealing from them, beating, assaulting, and even and lynching them. They wore white hoods to hide their faces.

The worst form of terror against black Americans was the practice of lynching. A white mob would gather and pretend that they were administering justice by hanging and burning a black person from a nearby tree. They usually accused the black person of a crime, but never gave him or her a fair trial. Most lynchings took place between 1890 and 1920, but it still happens today.[5] In fact, many scholars consider the instances of police killing unarmed young black men, such as the shooting of Michael Brown in Ferguson, Missouri, as a form of lynching as well. This killing spawned the creation of the Black Lives Matter movement, which spread across the country via cable news, and since then, citizens have been using the cameras on their cell phones to document many more instances of police violence on unarmed people.

VIEWS ON SLAVERY: IN THE WORDS OF ENSLAVED AFRICANS, MERCHANTS, OWNERS, AND ABOLITIONISTS

Under the oppressive Jim Crow laws, blacks could not drink from white water fountains, use white restrooms, sit in white theatres, or eat in white restaurants throughout the South.

"WE ARE THE CHANGE THAT WE SEEK"

JIM CROW

After slavery, new laws were quickly written. Called Jim Crow laws, they made sure that black laborers would still be under the thumb of the planters. Many former slaves still worked the same land, but now were farming as sharecroppers.

Some of these laws limited where blacks could buy or rent housing. Some laws, called vagrancy laws, forced blacks to work for plantation owners whether they wanted to or not. Blacks who quit their jobs could be arrested and jailed. Blacks could not testify in court against whites. A black person could be fined for making a speech that whites did not like or for insulting a white person. The worst of the laws took away a black person's right to vote in any election.[6]

Throughout the late nineteenth and most of the twentieth century, local Jim Crow laws were established to keep black Americans from living in the same neighborhoods as whites, from going to the same schools as whites, or from riding in the same railroad cars. Blacks were even banned from drinking out of the same water fountains as whites. This was called segregation.

CONTINUING THE FIGHT FOR FREEDOM

To curb these impulses by prejudiced whites, federal laws were passed during the 1960s that prohibited discrimination against people because of their race. These laws were called Civil Rights

VIEWS ON SLAVERY: IN THE WORDS OF ENSLAVED AFRICANS, MERCHANTS, OWNERS, AND ABOLITIONISTS

Nearly 100 years after slavery was abolished, the Civil Rights Movement took root in the United States. One of its most powerful leaders was Dr. Martin Luther King, Jr.

"WE ARE THE CHANGE THAT WE SEEK"

laws. They were enacted after many years of protests by blacks and whites needing federal government help. Like Frederick Douglass, Reverend Martin Luther King, Jr. realized that only political methods could affect needed reform. He knew that a person could not wait for the hearts and minds of whites to change. He even wrote in his famous "Letter from a Birmingham Jail": "Justice delayed is justice denied."

White beliefs about living equally with black Americans did not change even with new Civil Rights laws. As late as 2013, a poll taken by Rasmussen Reports revealed that only 30 percent of all Americans rated race relations as good or excellent; 14 percent thought that race relations were poor; 29 percent believed relations are getting better; and 32 percent felt it was getting worse. Thirty-five percent think race relations between blacks and whites are about the same. This report reveals a pessimism that is stunning.[7]

Sad facts today speak for themselves. More young black men end up in prison than enter college. Even though people of color make up only 30 percent of the population, 60 percent of individuals in prison are people of color. One in three black men will probably go to prison in his lifetime.[8]

VIEWS ON SLAVERY: IN THE WORDS OF ENSLAVED AFRICANS, MERCHANTS, OWNERS, AND ABOLITIONISTS

> In his "Letter From a Birmingham Jail," Martin Luther King Jr. declares that since African Americans overcame an institution as cruel as slavery, they can surely overcome the injustices of segregation:
>
> *For more than two centuries our forebears labored in this country without wages; . . . they built the homes of their masters while suffering gross injustice and shameful humiliation—and yet out of a bottomless vitality they continued to thrive and develop. If the inexpressible cruelties of slavery could not stop us, the opposition we now face will surely fail. We will win our freedom because the sacred heritage of our nation and the eternal will of God are embodied in our echoing demands.*[9]

Segregated inner-city public schools do not have enough textbooks for black students because mostly white state governments have financially starved these schools for decades, while suburban white schools enjoy more resources. Racial discrimination still exists in America's job scene. In August 2014, the unemployment rate for African-Americans was 11.4 percent, more than twice the rate of white unemployment (5.3 percent).[10] False beliefs of racial inferiority persist and continue to hurt African Americans and other people of color because public policy is primarily based on the views of whites.

All the different views of slavery in this book illustrate the diverse personalities who experienced it. From the theories of the polygenists like Le Conte to the abolitionists like Garrison and Douglass fighting for the end of slavery, people grew up believing certain things that mattered to them. These differing attitudes clashed on many levels until the Civil War finally ended slavery as a legal institution.

"WE ARE THE CHANGE THAT WE SEEK"

However, it did not immediately change the hearts and minds of white Americans. The end of slavery, though, did start a long march toward equality that continues today. Committed leaders like Frederick Douglass, Booker T. Washington, W. E. B. DuBois, and Martin Luther King, Jr. have created a legacy upon which modern African-American leaders have continued to build. Blacks and whites are talking more about their joint legacy of racism. Teachers are incorporating more ethnic histories into the mosaic of American culture than ever before. There is much to rejoice about, but there is much more work to be done.

TIMELINE

1517 Slave trading in the New World begins.

1621 Dutch West Indian Company is formed.

1672 English Royal African Company is formed.

1750 John Newton gets his own slave trading ship, the *Duke of Argyle*.

1755 Olaudah Equiano is captured in Africa around the age of ten; John Newton quits slave trading.

1766 Olaudah Equiano buys his freedom.

1797 Olaudah Equiano dies; William Lloyd Garrison is born.

1807 John Newton dies.

1813 Harriet Jacobs is born.

1815 Henry Bibb is born.

1818 Frederick Douglass is born.

1823 Joseph Le Conte is born.

1831 The first issue of *The Liberator* is published by William Lloyd Garrison.

1833 New England Anti-Slavery Society is established.

TIMELINE

1835 A mob takes over post office and destroys anti-slavery mail.

1839 *Amistad* revolt occurs.

1850 Fugitive Slave Act is passed.

1852 *Uncle Tom's Cabin* is published.

1854 Henry Bibb dies.

1855 Frederick Douglass writes essay "Three Kinds of Abolitionists."

1861 Civil War begins and Harriet Jacobs publishes *Incidents in the Life of a Slave Girl*, written by herself.

1863 Abraham Lincoln announces the Emancipation Proclamation.

1865 Civil War ends; Congress passes the Thirteenth Amendment.

1865 Ku Klux Klan is formed.

1866 Black Codes are passed in the South.

1875 Jim Crow laws are enacted in the South; William Lloyd Garrison dies.

1895 Letitia Burwell publishes her book *A Girl's Life in Virginia Before the War* (Birth and death dates for Burwell are unknown); Frederick Douglass dies.

1897 Harriet Jacobs dies.

1901 Joseph Le Conte dies.

1963 Dr. Martin Luther King, Jr.'s March on Washington occurs.

VIEWS ON SLAVERY: IN THE WORDS OF ENSLAVED AFRICANS, MERCHANTS, OWNERS, AND ABOLITIONISTS

<u>1964</u> Voting Rights Act is passed.

<u>1968</u> Fair Housing Act is passed.

<u>1994</u> President Bill Clinton signs the Violent Crime Control and Law Enforcement Act, which began the move toward the mass incarceration of young black men.

<u>2008</u> Barack Obama is elected President of the United States.

<u>2013</u> The United States Supreme Court strikes down a key part of the Voting Rights Act

<u>2014</u> Michael Brown is killed by police in Ferguson, Missouri and the Black Lives Matter movement begins.

CHAPTER NOTES

CHAPTER 1. ESCAPE TO FREEDOM

1. Henry Bibb, *Narrative of the Life and Adventures of Henry Bibb, an American Slave*, Written By Himself. (New York: Published by the Author, 1849), p. 64. Electronic Edition, "Documenting the American South," University of North Carolina at Chapel Hill Libraries, <http://docsouth.unc.edu/neh/bibb/bibb.html> December 15, 2015).
2. Ibid., p. 15.
3. Ibid., pp. 15–16.
4. Eugene D. Genovese, *Roll, Jordan, Roll: The World the Slaves Made*, (New York: Vintage Books, 1976), pp. 650–651.
5. Bibb, p. 33.
6. Genovese, p. 650.
7. Charles Joyner, "The World of Plantation Slaves," *Before Freedom Came: African-American Life in the Antebellum South*, (Charlottesville: University Press of Virginia, 1991), p. 60.
8. Bibb, p. 46.
9. Ibid., p. 25.
10. Genovese, p. 391.
11. Bibb, p. 55.
12. Ibid., p. 56.
13. Ibid., p. 59.
14. Genovese, p. 650.
15. John Hope Franklin and Alfred A. Moss Jr., *From Slavery to Freedom*, (New York: McGraw Hill, 1994), pp. 184–185.
16. Bibb, p. 65.
17. Ibid., pp. 67–68.
18. Ibid., p. 80.
19. Ibid., p. 86.
20. Ibid., p. 87.

VIEWS ON SLAVERY: IN THE WORDS OF ENSLAVED AFRICANS, MERCHANTS, OWNERS, AND ABOLITIONISTS

21. Ibid., p. 122.
22. Ibid., p. 124.
23. Ibid., p. 128.
24. Ibid., p. 147.
25. Ibid., p. xi.

CHAPTER 2. SLAVE MERCHANT TO AMAZING GRACE

1. John Newton, *The Journal of a Slave Trader*, eds. Bernard Martin and Mark Spurrell, (London: Epworth Press, 1962), p. x.
2. John Newton, The Works of Rev. John Newton. Vol. 1. 1808. Ulan Press: 2012, pg. 41.
3. Ibid.
4. Ibid.
5. Herbert S. Klein, *The Atlantic Slave Trade*, (London: Cambridge University Press, 1999), p. 79.
6. Newton, p. 9.
7. Ibid., p. xi.
8. Klein, p. 144.
9. "The Story of Africa," BBC World Service, n.d., <http://www.bbc.co.uk/worldservice/africa/features/ storyofafrica/9chapter5.shtml> (December 15, 2015).
10. Thomas Howard, ed. *Black Voyage: Eyewitness Accounts of the Atlantic Slave Trade*, (Boston: Little Brown and Company, 1971), p. 91.
11. Newton, p. 22.
12. Ibid., p. 29.
13. Ibid., p. 18.
14. Joseph Miller, "West Central Africa," The Atlantic Slave Trade, 2nd ed., ed. David Northrup, (Boston: Houghton Mifflin Co., 2002), p. 51.
15. John Newton, *"From Thoughts Upon the African Slave Trade," The Norton Anthology of English Literature: The Restoration and Eighteenth Century: Topics,* © 2003–2004, <http://www.wwnorton.com/

CHAPTER NOTES

nto/18ccntury/ topic_2/newton.htm > (December 15, 2015).
16. Ibid., p. 98.
17. Ibid., p. 99.

CHAPTER 3. GOODBYE TO AFRICA, MY HOME

1. Olaudah Equiano, *The Interesting Narrative and Other Writings*, (New York: Penguin Books, 1993), p. 32.
2. Ibid., p. 35.
3. Andrew Froiland, "Ibos People" http://www.africaguide.com/culture/tribes/ibo.htm (December 15, 2015).
4. Equiano, p. 34.
5. Froiland.
6. Equiano, p. 32.
7. Madeleine Burnside, *Spirits of Passage,* ed. Rosemarie Robotham (New York: Simon and Schuster, 1997), p. 27.
8. Equiano, p. 40.
9. Ibid., p. 54.
10. Ibid., p. 47.
11. Olaudah Equiano, *The Interesting Narrative of the Life of Olaudah Equiano, or Gustavus Vassa, the African*, Written by Himself, (London: Published by the author, 1789), vol. 1, pp. 247–249. Electronic Edition "Documenting the American South," University of North Carolina at Chapel Hill Libraries, <http://docsouth.unc.edu/neh/equiano1/equiano1.html> (December 15, 2015).
12. Equiano, *The Interesting Narrative and Other Writings*, p. 55.
13. Ibid.
14. Burnside, pp. 121–122.
15. Equiano, p. 56.
16. Ibid.
17. Ibid.
18. Ibid., p. 58.
19. Burnside, p. 122.

20. Equiano, p. 59.
21. Ibid., p. 60.
22. Vincent Carretta, "Introduction," Olaudah Equiano: The Interesting Narrative and Other Writings, (New York: Penguin Books, 1993), p. ix.

CHAPTER 4. SCIENCE AND RACISM

1. Joseph Le Conte, *The Autobiography of Joseph Le Conte,* ed. William Dallam Armes (New York: D. Appleton and Co., 1901), p. 9.
2. Ibid.
3. Ibid., p. 23.
4. Ibid., pp. 12–13.
5. "The Idea of Race," n.d., "One Race or Several Species" <http://www.understandingrace.org/history/science/one_race.html> (December 15, 2015).
6. Winthrop D. Jordan, *White Over Black: American Attitudes Toward the Negro 1550–1812*, (Chapel Hill: University of North Carolina Press, 1968), p. 7.
7. Le Conte, p. 13.
8. Jordan, pp. 432–433.
9. Ibid., p. 437.
10. Joseph Le Conte, "The Race Problem in the South," *Man and State: studies in applied sociology; popular lectures and discussions before the Brooklyn ethical association*, (New York: D. Appleton and Co., 1892), p. 367.
11. Philip Morgan, "Three Planters and their Slaves," *Race and Family in the Colonial South*, eds. Winthrop D. Jordan and Sheila L. Skemp (Jackson, Mississippi: University Press of Mississippi, 1987), p. 40.
12. John W. Blassingame, *The Slave Community: Plantation Life in the Antebellum South*, (New York: Oxford University Press, 1979), p. 256.
13. Ibid., p. 161.
14. Le Conte, *The Autobiography of Joseph Le Conte*, p. 215.

CHAPTER NOTES

15. Frederick Douglass, "The Slave's Right to Steal," *Frederick Douglass: The Narrative and Selected Writings*, (New York: McGraw Hill, 1984), p. 136.
16. James C. Scott, *Domination and the Arts of Resistance*, (New Haven: Yale University Press, 1990), pp. 10–11.
17. Le Conte, "The Race Problem in the South," p. 376.
18. thenation.com/article/supreme-court-eviscerates-voting-rights-act-texas-voter-id-decision/ -December 14, 2015
19. http://www.ourdocuments.gov/doc.php?doc=100&page=transcript.

CHAPTER 5. PAMPERED BLINDNESS

1. Letitia M. Burwell, "A Girl's Life in Virginia Before the War," Electronic Edition. *University of North Carolina at Chapel Hill Libraries. Documenting the American South.* (1895) Dedication <http://docsouth.unc.edu/fpn/burwell/burwell.html> (December 15, 2015).
2. Ibid., pp. 2–3.
3. Elizabeth Fox-Genovese, *Within the Plantation Household: Black and White Women of the Old South*, (Chapel Hill: University of North Carolina Press, 1988), p. 81.
4. Ibid., p. 109.
5. Burwell, p. 4.
6. Fox-Genovese, p. 114.
7. Burwell, p. 6.
8. Fox-Genovese, p. 137.
9. Eugene Genovese, *Roll, Jordan, Roll: The World the Slaves Made*, (New York: Random House, 1974), p. 344.
10. Burwell, pp. 128–129.
11. Ibid., pp. 158–159.
12. Ibid., p. 162.
13. Ruef, Martin. *Between Slavery and Capitalism: The Legacy of Emancipation In the American South.* Princeton University Press: 2014, pg. 95.

14. Burwell, pp. 163–164.
15. Ibid., p. 44.

CHAPTER 6. DESPERATE TO LIVE FREE

1. Harriet A. Jacobs, *Incidents in the Life of a Slave Girl*, (Cambridge: Harvard University Press, 1987), p. 114.
2. Ibid.
3. Edward W. Phifer, "Slavery in Microcosm: Burke County, North Carolina," *Plantation, Town and Country*, eds. Elinor Miller and Eugene D. Genovese (Chicago: University Press of Illinois, 1974), p. 83.
4. Jacobs, p. 6.
5. Ibid., p. 7.
6. Ibid., p. 8.
7. Ibid., p. 9.
8. Ibid., p. 12.
9. Ibid.
10. Ibid., p. 27.
11. Elizabeth Fox-Genovese, *Within the Plantation Household: Black and White Women of the Old South*, (Chapel Hill: University of North Carolina Press, 1988), p. 39.
12. Jacobs, p. 99.
13. Ibid., p. 104.
14. Ibid., p. 105.
15. Ibid., p. 109.
16. Ibid.
17. Ibid., p. 111.
18. Ibid., p. 113.
19. Ibid., p. 115.
20. Ibid., p. 158.
21. Judith S. Levey and Agnes Greenhall, eds., *The Concise Columbia Encyclopedia*, (New York: Columbia University Press, 1983), p. 312.

CHAPTER NOTES

22. Jacobs, p. 199.
23. Harriet Jacobs, *Incidents in the Life of a Slave Girl*, ed. L. Maria Child (Boston: Published for the author, 1861), p. 114. "Documenting the American South," University of North Carolina at Chapel Hill Libraries, 2003, <http://docsouth.unc.edu/fpn/jacobs/jacobs.html> (December 15, 2015).

CHAPTER 7. FREEDOM'S HEROES

1. Frederick Douglass, "Narrative of the Life of Frederick Douglass: An American Slave," *Frederick Douglass: The Narrative and Selected Writings*, (New York: Random House, 1984), p. 11.
2. William Lloyd Garrison, "To the Public," *The Liberator,* January 1, 1831. David W. Blight, "Africans in America," n.d., <http://www.pbs.org/wgbh/aia/part4/4p1561.html> (December 15, 2015).
3. Michael Meyer, "Introduction," *Frederick Douglass: The Narrative and Selected Writings*, (New York: Random House, 1984), pp. 10–11.
4. David W. Blight, "Africans in America," <http://www.pbs.org/wgbh/aia.part4/4p1561.html> (December 15, 2015).
5. Frederick Douglass, *Life and Times of Frederick Douglass*, (New York: Gramercy Books, 1993), pp. 180–181.
6. Frederick Douglass, "The Liberator and William Garrison," *Frederick Douglass: The Narrative and Selected Writings*, (New York: Random House, 1984), pp. 154–155.
7. Frederick Douglass, "The Liberator and William Garrison," p. 159.
8. Frederick Douglass, *Narrative of the Life of Frederick Douglass, an American Slave*. Written by Himself (Boston: Published At The Anti-Slavery Office, No. 25 Cornhill, 1845), p. 19. Electronic Edition, "Documenting the American South, University of North Carolina at Chapel Hill Libraries, 1999, <http://docsouth.unc.edu/neh/douglass/douglass.html> (December 15, 2015).
9. Frederick Douglass, *The Mind and Heart of Frederick Douglass: Excerpts from Speeches of the Great Negro Orator*, ed., Barbara Ritchie (New York: Thomas Y. Crowell Company, 1968), pp. 17–18.

VIEWS ON SLAVERY: IN THE WORDS OF ENSLAVED AFRICANS, MERCHANTS, OWNERS, AND ABOLITIONISTS

10. Douglass, "The Liberator and William Garrison," p. 160.
11. John Hope Franklin, *From Slavery to Freedom*, (New York: McGraw Hill, 1994), pp. 1973–1974.
12. William E. Cain and Alfred A. Moss Jr., *William Lloyd Garrison and the Fight Against Slavery: Selections from the Liberator*, (Boston: St. Martin's Press, 1995), p. 150.
13. Blight.
14. Richard Rudderman, Ashbrook Colloqium, "Frederick Douglass and William Lloyd Garrison," <http://ashbrook.org/podcast/richard-ruderman-frederick-douglass-and-william-lloyd-garrison/> (December 15, 2015).
15. Frederick Douglass, "Various Incidents," *Frederick Douglass: The Narrative and Selected Writings*, (New York: Random House, 1984), p. 166.
16. George M. Fredrickson, ed. William Lloyd Garrison, (Englewood, NJ: Prentice-Hall, 1968), p. 92.
17. Frederick Douglass, "Various Incidents," *Frederick Douglass: The Narrative and Selected Writings*, p. 167.
18. Ibid., p. 353.
19. Ibid., p. 355.
20. Ibid., p. 357.
21. Ibid.
22. Ibid., p. 358.
23. Eric Foner, "On the Abolitionist Movement," *Africans in America*, n.d., <http://www.pbs.org/wgbh/aia/part4/4i2974.html> (December 15, 2015).
24. William Scarborough, "On the South and the Abolitionist Movement," *Africans in America*, n.d., <http://www.pbs.org/wgbh/aia/part4/4i2979.html> (December 15, 2015).
25. Cain, p. 152.
26. Frederick Douglass, "Abolitionist Lecturer," *Frederick Douglass: The Narrative and Selected Writings*, p. 168.
27. Douglass, *The Mind and Heart of Frederick Douglass*, p. 128.

CHAPTER NOTES

28. Cain, pp. 182–183.

CHAPTER 8. "WE ARE THE CHANGE THAT WE SEEK"

1. "Barack Obama's Feb. 5 Speech," *New York Times,* Feb, 5, 2008, http://www.nytimes.com/2008/02/05/us/politics/05text-obama.html?_r=0 (April 11, 2016).
2. David Dabydeen, "Poetic Licence," *The Guardian*, http://www.theguardian.com/books/2005/dec/03/featuresreviews.guardianreview3 (December 2, 2005).
3. Boulukos, George E. "Olaudah Equiano and the Eighteenth-Century Debate on Africa," *Eighteenth-Century Studies* Vol. 40, No. 2 (Winter, 2007), pp. 241–255.
4. William Z. Foster, *The Negro People In American History*, (New York: International Publishers, 1973), p. 327.
5. Danny Postel, "The Awful Truth: Lynching in America," Znet, n.d., <https://zcomm.org/znetarticle/the-awful-truth-lynching-in-america-by-danny-postel/> (December 15, 2015).
6. John Hope Franklin and Alfred A. Moss Jr., *From Slavery to Freedom*, 7th ed., (New York: McGraw Hill, 1994), p. 225.
7. http://www.rasmussenreports.com/public_content/lifestyle/general_lifestyle/july_2013/more_americans_view_blacks_as_racist_than_whites_hispanics - December 14, 2015
8. Sophia Kerby, "The Top 10 Most Startling Facts About People of Color and Criminal Justice in the United States" Center for American Progress, <https://www.americanprogress.org/issues/race/news/2012/03/13/11351/the-top-10-most-startling-facts-about-people-of-color-and-criminal-justice-in-the-united-states/> (March 13, 2012).
9. Martin Luther King, Jr., "Letter From a Birmingham Jail," *University of Pennsylvania—African Studies Center*, n.d., <http://www.africa.upenn.edu/Articles_Gen/Letter_Birmingham.html> (December 15, 2015).

VIEWS ON SLAVERY: IN THE WORDS OF ENSLAVED AFRICANS, MERCHANTS, OWNERS, AND ABOLITIONISTS

10. Philip Bump, "Black Unemployment Is Always Much Worse Than White Unemployment. But the Gap Depends on Where You Live," *Washington Post*, <https://www.washingtonpost.com/news/the-fix/wp/2014/09/06/black-unemployment-is-always-much-worse-than-white-unemployment-but-the-gap-depends-on-where-you-live/> (September 6, 2014).

GLOSSARY

abolitionist—A person who favored ending slavery.

antebellum—Latin word meaning "before the war." In this case, the American Civil War.

chattel—Property.

coasting period—The months spent along the coast of Africa buying slaves to fill the holds of the slave ships.

discrimination—Showing intolerance toward people who are different than the majority.

entrepreneur—A person who starts his or her own business.

Jim Crow laws—Laws on the state and local level that enforced segregation and effectively oppressed African-American citizens.

longboats—The largest boats carried by the slave ships.

Middle Passage—The route where slaves were carried from the coast of Africa to America or the West Indies.

overseer—A white man hired by a slave owner to manage and watch the slaves on a plantation.

paternalism—The view that Southern planters should keep order and authority on their land at all times by insisting on complete obedience from the slaves and, for the most part, their wives and daughters.

polygenism—The theory that there is more than one human race and that they are of differing origins.

VIEWS ON SLAVERY: IN THE WORDS OF ENSLAVED AFRICANS, MERCHANTS, OWNERS, AND ABOLITIONISTS

segregation—Forced separation of racial groups.

sharecroppers—After the Civil War, people who would work a planter's farm in return for a percentage of the crop.

slave trader—A captain of a slave ship that transported slaves to America and the West Indies.

triangle trade—The route taken by ships, from England to Africa to North America, that involved the delivering of cargo, including slaves.

Underground Railroad—A secret set of connections set up by black and white abolitionists to aid slaves escaping from the South.

FURTHER READING

BOOKS

Burgan, Michael. *African Americans in the Thirteen Colonies.* New York: Children's Press, 2013.

Ford, Carin T. *The Underground Railroad and Slavery Through Primary Sources.* Berkeley Heights, NJ: Enslow, 2013.

Holzer, Harold. *Lincoln: How Abraham Lincoln Ended Slavery in America.* New York, NY: Newmarket Press for It Books, an imprint of HarperCollins Publishers, 2013.

Marsico, Katie. *Slavery: A Chapter in American History.* Vero Beach, FL: Rourke Educational Media, 2014.

Moretta, Alison. *Legal Debates of the Antislavery Movement.* New York, NY: Cavendish Square Publishing, 2016.

Muldoon, Kathleen M. *The Jim Crow Era.* North Mankato, MN: ABDO Publishing Company, 2015.

Northup, Solomon. *Twelve Years a Slave.* Engage Books: 2013.

Shea, Nicole. *Frederick Douglass in His Own Words.* New York, NY: Gareth Stevens Publishing, 2014.

Wells, Catherine. *Slavery and the Forging of Early America.* Greensboro, NC: Morgan Reynolds Publsihing, 2015.

Winch, Julie. *Between Slavery and Freedom.* Lanham, MD: Rowan and Littlefield Publishers, 2014.

Yancey, Diane. *The Abolition of Slavery.* San Diego, CA: ReferencePoint Press, 2013.

VIEWS ON SLAVERY: IN THE WORDS OF ENSLAVED AFRICANS, MERCHANTS, OWNERS, AND ABOLITIONISTS

WEBSITES

American Slave Anthology
xroads.virginia.edu/~hyper/wpa/wpahome.html
This fascinating online resource features slave narratives and resources for learning more about slavery's history in America.

Library of Congress: African American Odessey
lcweb2.loc.gov/ammem/aaohtml/
This site features primary source narrative, images, and video telling the story of African Americans in the United States.

National Underground Railroad Freedom Center
www.freedomcenter.org/
This museum celebrates freedom by telling the stories of those involved in the Underground Railroad.

INDEX

A

abolitionists, 13, 17, 19, 44, 54, 78–79, 81, 87–88, 92–93, 99, 106
Africa, 19, 21, 25, 30, 35–39, 96
Aunt Fanny, 64–65

B

Benin, 33, 96
Bibb, Henry, 7–17, 96, 99
Bibb, Malinda, 11, 13, 16–17
Bibb, Mary Frances, 11, 16–17
"Big House," 60, 66
Black Lives Matter, 100, 101
"bloody flux," 30
Brown, Michael, 101

C

Canada, 8, 9, 13
Christianity, 85
civil rights, 94, 103–105
Civil War, 19, 53, 57, 64–65, 81, 88, 92, 99, 106
"coasting period," 25, 27, 30, 39
Constitution, 87
　as antislavery document, 87–88, 92

D

Daddy Dick, 45
discrimination, 56, 103, 106
Douglass, Frederick, 54, 79, 80–85, 87–93, 95, 99, 105–107
"down river," 13
Dutch West India Company, 23

E

Emancipation Proclamation, 93
English Royal African Company, 23
Equiano, Olaudah, 32, 33–44, 96, 99

F

Flint, Dr., 67, 70–72, 76, 78
Free Soil Party, 88
Fugitive Slave Act, 76, 87

G

Garrison, William Lloyd, 79, 80–81, 85–88, 90, 92, 93, 99, 106
Garrisonian Abolitionists, 88, 90, 92
"Great Chain of Being, The," 48

VIEWS ON SLAVERY: IN THE WORDS OF ENSLAVED AFRICANS, MERCHANTS, OWNERS, AND ABOLITIONISTS

I

Ibo, 33, 35, 44

J

Jacobs, Harriet, 66, 67–79, 97
Jefferson, Thomas, 50
Jim Crow laws, 103
"jumping the broom," 11

K

King, Martin Luther, Jr., 104–107
Ku Klux Klan, 98, 99

L

Le Conte, Joseph, 45–54, 97, 106
Liberator, The, 79, 81, 83, 85, 86, 90, 93
Lincoln, Abraham, 93, 99
Louisiana, 13, 15, 16, 85
Lovejoy, Elijah, 92
lynching, 101

M

Middle Passage, 25, 30, 32, 39

N

Newton, John, 21–32, 95, 96
New England Anti-Slavery Society, 76, 85

New York, 72
Norcom, James. See Flint, Dr.
North Star, 88

O

Obama, Barack, 95

P

Paternalism, 51, 56, 59, 66, 71, 97
Philadelphia, Pa., 76, 79
plantations, 9, 57, 71, 78,
   Burwell, 59
   Gatewood, 11, 12, 13
   Otterburn, 64
   Woodmanston, 46
polygenism, 46, 48–49, 54, 97, 106

Q

Quakers, 76, 79

R

racism, 97, 107
Radical Abolitionists, 88, 92
Republican Party, 88

S

segregation, 103, 106
sharecroppers, 103
Sherman, William T., 53

INDEX

slaveholders, 9, 11–13, 17, 19, 25, 27, 46, 51, 53–54, 57–69, 71, 78, 81–83, 87, 92, 97, 99
slave hunters, 9, 13, 16
slavery
   in America, 35–36
   in the British colonies, 17
   chattel, 17
   conditions aboard slave ships, 19, 25, 27–31, 38–40, 96
   escape, 9, 12–17, 53, 74, 76, 81, 97
   happiness of slaves, 46–48, 51–53, 59, 87, 97
   legacy of, 20, 107
   mistreatment of slaves, 9, 35, 38, 43, 46, 50, 57, 69, 70–71
   religious beliefs of slaves, 25, 65
   resistance to, 40, 54
   slave traders, 25, 30, 31, 39, 40, 72, 78, 96
   white blindness to cruelty of, 31–32, 57–66, 96
southern culture, 56, 59

religion, 65
resistance to abolitionists, 92–93
slave/mistress relationship, 60–64
white slaveholding women, 56, 57–59, 65–66

T

Thirteenth Amendment, 17
triangular trade, 19, 25–26

U

Underground Railroad, 13, 88

V

vagrancy laws, 103
voting, 54, 88, 103
Voting Rights Act of 1965, 55–56

W

Wheatley, Phillis, 50